BAPTIST GUILT

ROBERTA PERSINGER MANN

WestBow Press books may be ordered through booksellers or by contacting:

WestBow Press
A Division of Thomas Nelson & Zondervan
1663 Liberty Drive
Bloomington, IN 47403
www.westbowpress.com
1 (866) 928-1240

Scripture taken from the King James Version of the Bible.

ISBN: 978-1-9736-8966-9 (sc)
ISBN: 978-1-9736-8968-3 (hc)
ISBN: 978-1-9736-8967-6 (e)

Library of Congress Control Number: 2020907059

Print information available on the last page.

WestBow Press rev. date: 04/28/2020

ACKNOWLEDGEMENTS

This book is dedicated to the memory of my dear aunt: Patricia Ellen Canterbury Boone "Patty," "whom we loved, but could not save."

"Special thank you to my loving mother Eva Burdette for your guidance throughout the years."

"Thank you, Dr. Rhonda L. Hamm D.O. for your role as both clinician and friend."

"Thanks also to my friend Mary A. Fox, without whom this book would have no title."

"Thank you to my uncle Stan Eller for fostering my love for horses."

INTRODUCTION

This book was written in order to share with readers there is hope in overcoming bouts of depression and anxiety. Specifically using the teaching of God's Holy Bible to encourage and uplift fellow believers who may be feeling less than themselves. This book was designed to speak to not only those suffering from depression, but to others as well. The audience consists of Christian leaders, family, friends, and coworkers who may have difficulty understanding the illness and what it is doing to their loved one. It offers ways to support and not condemn the person experiencing those feelings. The religious sects and its counterparts often place such a stigma on mental illness. This can be very detrimental for the victim to accept the fact they are suffering, and more importantly to get the help they need. This book will hopefully break down those walls between religion and mental illness. We as Christians must learn to love and to not condemn, just as Christ himself has done. Sometimes being told anxiety is sin by spiritual leaders will produce the natural response of denial. Thus, allowing the darkness of depression to send fellow believers "over the edge." This short revelation is designed to let others suffering from depression know they are not alone. God loves them and will never leave them in their helpless state.

CHAPTER 1

IN THE BEGINNING

I guess you might say I was born into sorrow. The year was 1971 and our nation was in the throes of a terrible war in Vietnam. A small town in rural West Virginia was ripped apart and reeling with the loss of so many young men, as were many small towns and cities across the United States. My momma, raised on a tiny farm at the foot of a large mountain called Keeney's Knob, had just gotten the worst news of her young life. Twenty years old and eight months pregnant, she found herself alone and without the love of her life. Daddy was only twenty-two when his chopper was riddled with bullets over the Vietnamese jungle. Drafted early on, he attended flight school, and promised a quick tour, which would soon reunite him with his growing family. Unfortunately, after only a few months as a warrant officer, this up-and-coming pilot was struck by enemy fire. He spent two weeks in a field hospital, but soon fell ill with an infection that ended his young life. A man who was praised for his kindness, generosity, and his love of God and family was gone. A pilot whose crew loved and depended on his calm quiet demeanor in the heat of battle was lost in a whisper. My father, my hero.

Deeply saddened with the loss, but given no time to grieve, my young mother soon went into labor only twenty-five days after the horrific tragedy. Dropped off by my grandparents who were busy taking care of the family farm in addition to seven other children, she was left alone to deliver. The nurses were kind under the circumstances and remained by her side as she delivered a healthy baby girl. When the angels in white asked for the name, it was the name Daddy had chosen. The feminine version of his own name Robert.

Despite the early years of overcoming the grief and memories of a love lost, my momma made certain I had a happy childhood. I was perfectly content growing up on granddaddy's farm. Nestled in a sheltered little hollow-or-holler as we say, I didn't even wonder about the outside world. Playing in the creek, wandering in the woods, and frolicking in the fields on the farm was absolute bliss. I enjoyed going over to my best friend's place and getting into mischief. Her daddy had an even larger farm, we raised hogs, they raised cattle. We spent our days playing house in the barn loft or pretending to be truckers in the old truck her daddy kept on the farm. What an imagination we had, we practically lived outside. From gathering eggs, to sampling raw maple syrup, I felt like I was on top of the world.

One visit I remember, she and I had gotten bored with all the usual antics. We decided to go for a walk and let her young cousin from the city tag along. As you can imagine we were thrilled when we found a large embankment beside of her incredibly long driveway, covered in red dirt. As country girls we are taught early that "God made dirt and dirt can't hurt." We climbed to the top and begin taking turns sliding down that steep bank. Dust was rolling in that mid-summer heat. We were laughing and having a ball, until city girl snurled up her nose and ran to my friend's momma to tattle. Of course, we were in a good bit of trouble when the cousin showed up still in her pristine state of cleanliness, and we looked as if we had been buried alive. Her momma came after us and made us strip at the back door. Next thing we know we were back to back in that big ole tub of hers scrubbing for the better part of an hour. I can remember vividly, climbing out, looking over my shoulder and seeing about two inches worth of mud in the bottom. Her poor momma spent the better part of the evening bleaching the entire bathroom. I so enjoyed my time spent at their farm. They were all like a second family to me.

Of course, church was an early and precious memory that I still hold dear. I had two wonderful Sunday school teachers, who laid the foundation for my love for God and our savior Jesus Christ. They were staunch gray-haired sisters who shared not only a love for the Lord, but also the children who were entrusted to their care. I remember the "dinners on the ground," vacation Bible school, and revivals, all held in a small country church less than a mile and a half from our farm. Notice I mentioned-dinners on the ground-first, a good indication I was raised in the Baptist faith. A play on a very familiar and wonderful verse and my favorite Baptist meme; "Where two or three Baptists are gathered together-a chicken must die". So true though, Baptists make some of the best cooks. Martha Stewarts with a touch of "hillbilly charm" in my neck of the woods. Seriously though, my rural Baptist roots are primarily what shaped every aspect of my being. God is my Father and His Son "Jesus the author and finisher of my faith." (Hebrews 12:2) I wouldn't have it any other way.

Now a curveball, so to speak. After eight years of raising a "toe-headed-monster" my momma found someone. At first, of course, I was apprehensive. I did not wish to share the woman who had been the absolute center of my world. My grandparents, whom I adored, were also highly involved in my raising. I have to say that they taught me so much about life, love, and having an incredibly strong work ethic. Weren't they enough? I believe at this point, however, God thought it was high time I found out that the world didn't revolve around little ole me. But this stranger was not part of my original plan. Of course, I was spoiled and used to getting what I wanted. Who didn't feel sorry for the little war orphan, and in turn shower me with attention? Although we didn't have a lot of money, I was pretty set with what I had, not counting the people I had wrapped around my little finger. This was a total shock to my system. A man I barely knew was spending more and more time at the farm. He was taking my mother out on dates and leaving me with the grands. What?

But I will say this. He was the answer to my momma's prayers. He not only loved and supported my mother, but instantly became a father figure to me. He never tried to take Daddy's place, but he did one fine job of being a mentor and applying discipline and structure to my life. He showed me unconditional love even though I was not his own. Four decades later I'm still calling him Dad. If he taught me anything, it is being faithful to the God we serve. He quickly renewed his faith and came to church with us after he and Momma were married. He is still to this day attending, even with multiple health issues, each time the church doors are open.

So instead of no siblings I happily acquired two older brothers, both now retired from the military. I'm proud of their service to our country. Later, soon after my momma and new dad were married, I was even further blessed with a baby brother, who I love dearly. Nine years his senior I suppose I was somewhat of a mother figure in his life, that is when we weren't fighting. He has grown into an amazing father and husband, successful in all areas of his life. Most importantly, he never lost his faith, and currently serves in a large community church in a small suburb near Dallas Texas. A praise and worship leader, his musical talent is being used as God intended. I'm so proud of his successes in life, but especially proud of his service to our Lord and Savior. God is good. And He has blessed our family tremendously.

As I grew and completed my early years in school, then later college, I realized there actually was a big old world out there. It was a wakeup call for a little sheltered country girl to say the least. I must admit there were many things happening that I had never seen in my rural upbringing. West Virginia University was considered a "party school" and my acceptance was met with reproach from some of my spiritual leaders. They felt a Christian based school with a strictly Biblical curriculum would be ideal. I do not dispute the importance of attending such schools, and I do believe God has appointed certain students to thrive in those programs. I respected their opinions and knew in my heart that they only wanted the best for me, however, I had a completely different perspective. I felt strongly that being a Christian meant being so in any environment. The KJV Bible states "we are to be in the world, but not of the world." (John 15:19)

Now you may wonder what is the purpose behind entering a world that does not always support the Christian faith? My answer is this: to do the command of the Father. Did Jesus not commission his disciples in Mark 16:15, to "Go ye into all the world, and preach the gospel to every creature." I realize that most believers feel they need to shield their children from peer pressure and sinful influence. In this day and time, the detrimental effects of sin, can and will sometimes happen. This is where faith comes in. God also speaks to us from the book of Proverbs chapter 22, verse 6; "Train up a child in the way he should go: and when he is old, he will not depart from it." I wholeheartedly believe this promise. Even though my husband and I were never in God's plan to be blessed with children of our own, I've seen fellow Christians succeed by raising some truly amazing kids. Being a long time Sunday School teacher and former youth leader, I have seen examples of this many times over. We all need to pray and then let go to let God lead in an individual's life. Trust in God's hand to lead your child to be a light to others in his or her little corner of the world. I only pray that those of us who left Morgantown educated with world class academics, also left knowing we shared a little of God's love to those who may not have known it otherwise. Let's Go Mountaineers!

I suppose this book is a type of autobiography, not written to overshadow the Almighty God in all His power and might. Instead it stands as a testimony to what God can do for and through you in His service. I'm sure most of you understand the trinity. God the Father, (our Creator), God the Son, (Our Savior) and The Holy Spirit, (Our comforter). All three are there to help us grow and be successful as Christians. Please bear with me as I stumble through my first attempt at book writing. My life is not exciting by any means, but through my experience I have learned contentment, gratefulness, and forgiveness. Striving to follow our Lord and Savior, and prayerfully sharing with you what He has laid on my heart. I sincerely hope that this humble expression will help you the reader understand that you are not alone. My desire is this, to be pleasing to God and to help others suffering from the tyranny of depression.

CHAPTER 2

THRIVING AND SURVIVING

Now here is in this next stage of my life is where I make my point. Or more importantly where God makes His point. I grew to realize that time marches on. I had become a college graduate and married my high school sweetheart. I became eager to begin a career in healthcare because caring for others has always been my niche. My time at the university yielded a Bachelor of Science degree in nursing. A profession in which I wholeheartedly believe is designed by God himself. First commandment is to love God, but the Bible resonates time and time again to "love thy neighbor as thyself." (Mark 12:31) The field of nursing requires a close intimate means of caring for those you know, as well as complete strangers you've never even met. My first nursing job took place in an unfamiliar setting. The love of my life had decided in order to make a living he needed to serve in the United States army. So, travel became a must. Prior to my nursing graduation, he was assigned to a small base in Germany. We spent six months to a year apart more than once. That was extremely difficult for a young couple so much in love.

A portion of his time served in the early nineties was during the

"Desert Storm" excursion. A fearful time in my life, especially due to past circumstances, I learned to trust God even more. Who else could reach across an ocean and protect someone I had planned to spend my life with? But did I trust enough? My grades along with my emotional state soon deteriorated. My prayers consisted of, "Lord please don't let history repeat itself". First my father taken far too soon, now my fiancé, soon to be husband's life may be in jeopardy. God heard my cries. After only a few months of being on high alert, I was sitting in a Physiology lecture. I remember that blessed day well. As my professor was delivering her instruction, a messenger walked in and whispered in her ear. She looks up, smiles broadly, and announces that the military operation was over. I could breathe!!!

Getting back to the topic at hand I spent my first year as a nurse in a large but beautiful city, Colorado Springs. If you're like me and not a fan of cities, this one would be one to consider for sure. Nestled in the beauty of the Rockies, you could see Pikes Peak from our apartment just off the base at Fort Carson. It was a time of learning for me. A time where I could become who I thought God wanted me to be. Raised to be independent, adjusting to life as a wife was challenging. Sharing all things was a new habit for me. I had lived alone while in college and had my own routine. My husband had one of his own. Finally, the twain learned to meet in the middle. But not without a few spats here and there. A new job requiring double shifts, gave me a hard dose of reality.

I began realizing that adulting isn't all it's cracked up to be. Some folks, unfortunately, do not have the work ethic that others do. Lesson learned there. You can become burnt out relatively quickly when you find yourself working your designated nights, days, and weekends along with everyone else's. Thankfully, not everyone shares that trait of "maybe I'll work today and maybe

I won't." I've had role models and mentors in every aspect of my career. People engineered by God to come swiftly to my rescue, for encouragement, advice, and support. I am very thankful for each, and every nurse who has been my guide throughout the years. I really don't know what I would have down without them.

It was during this time in the early days of my career that I discovered a valuable teaching. Treat others how you would want to be treated. Wow, hmm, where have I heard that before? The Golden Rule, did that come from all my years of watching Little House on the Prairie? No, it's Biblical. Yes, Luke 6:31 tells us; "And as ye would that men should do to you, do ye also to them likewise." There it is in my opinion the secret of a happy successful life. God's simple way of helping us relate to others right there in that beautiful book we call the Bible. I practice this with all my young nurses, as well as everyone else I encounter. Not to say I always get it right, but with God's design it has given me the leadership role I have today.

My first year of marriage, in addition to working hard, taught me stewardship. God speaks of being a good steward often in the Old and New Testament. Steward as defined as someone to look after another's property or money. Did you know that what we consider "our money," is not actually ours but God's? That's right, He blesses us with the gifts we receive here on earth. Although my husband and I had very different views related to "spending," we were able to save a portion of my paycheck in order to prepare for our return home. Neither of us are the traveling type, both "homebody's," so to speak. We learned right away we were not cut out to be a military couple. I'm so thankful for those who are willing to risk their lives for this country. I'm also grateful to their families who give up the comfort of having their loved one home in safety. God Bless our military men and women, where would we be without them?

Did I thank God enough for allowing us to move back to our beloved state of West Virginia? I sometimes wonder if I appreciated the fact that only after a couple years of working and saving, God allowed us to purchase family land, plant a home, and create a small farm of our own. I say that because later I will reveal that a portion of my downfall, my weakness, shamefully is related to money and the accumulation of earthly possessions. I'm getting to that.

Once home we quickly settled into our routine life as Appalachian Americans. Some try to hide the fact that they are mountain folk, but others of us embrace it. Why not? We are after all a sheltered population who live in a slower paced peaceful society, where everyone knows everyone, and people look after their neighbors. What's not to love? God blessed us and we began to prosper. Work, family, homelife going well, until it didn't. I'm getting to that too; be patient. Patience, another huge lesson learned. Stay tuned.

CHAPTER 3

DOWNHILL

Ahh yes life was good. Career moving forward, happy marriage, enjoying family and friends, until one day the news came. My husband and I had been trying for several years to have children, but to no avail. We had tried somewhat conservative trials, hormonal treatments, and testing, but we were unsuccessful. Nothing happened. I chalked it up to God's plan for us, and tried pretending it was okay, but deep down I knew my heart had taken a hit. Oh sure, we thought about all the options. Adoption just didn't seem to be a fit for us, and neither did any of the artificial means. Coasting along, I became determined that my life would mean something. I became a manager and leader in the workplace. I re-joined former passions such as playing on the women's softball league, teaching Sunday School, and participating in community activities such as "John Henry Days."

Yes, I currently reside in Talcott, WV, where the John Henry Legend originated. For those of you who did not know this piece of American folklore, it is a true story. The story goes that a young black man working for the railroad, helped to fashion the Big Bend tunnel. This rather large tunnel allowed the train to pass through the Appalachian hillside. He died on that tragic day challenging a steam drill to a duel, where he would muster brute strength to defeat the machine that threatened their livelihood. He won the event, only to suffer what appeared to be a tragic heart attack. Being a history buff, I thought I would share that story of our small-town hero. You're welcome.

Let's see, where was I? Oh yes, my childlessness took deeper root than I cared to acknowledge. I kept going back to the Bible story of Hannah and how she prayed for a son. I prayed, I cried, I wondered what have a done wrong to deserve this barrenness. I know God revealed time and time again, that he could overcome any form of family issues. I thought of Sarah, Abrahams wife, in her nineties when God kept His promise and she bore Isaac. I also thought of Elizabeth also stricken with age, when God presented her with His messenger John. John was renowned for his declaration of the coming Savior, Jesus. Whoa, to be a mom and to have wildly successful children, that dear friends would be my dream come true. Sadly, it just wasn't in God's plan.

I genuinely tried to move through life pretending not to care about our situation. After all, I had my career, my church kids, my fur kids, and my big kid-the hubby. My life was full, or so I thought. Eventually the loss or lack thereof wore my spirit down and I could feel myself developing unhealthy habits. I began obsessing over little issues that seemed meaningless to some. For example, my fur kids began to take the place of actual children. I would go out late at night to make certain all the gates were closed to the kennels and the pasture. Yes, I am a huge animal lover, always have been and always will be. I would worry incessantly over their illnesses. So much so that I literally turned my pantry at the house into what appeared to be the livestock medicinal aisle at the local feed store. I know most all of Americans love their pets, but I was a bit ridiculous. People began to take notice. I looked tired, feeling anxious and seemed stressed. Folks could take one look at me and know something was up. A word to the wise, you never want me as a Poker partner. My facial expressions tell all.

As I mentioned before in biblical times and even some places still today, barren women were treated as less than desirable compared to their counterparts. Luke 1:25 states; "Thus hath the Lord dealt with me in the days wherein he looked on me, to take away my reproach among men." Yes Elisabeth, God created a miracle in your womb, happy day! Hey what was that you mentioned a reproach? Yikes! Reproach is defined as the expression of disapproval or disappointment. I began to wonder, am I a disappointment to my spouse, my family, myself? A hard question that I had refused to answer up to this point. I'm a type A personality, a Martha, not a Mary, unfortunately. I thrive on success and enjoy being the person everyone looks to for solutions when problems arise. Certainly, pregnancy was not an attainable goal for me, would I be viewed as a reproach by my peers? This was one issue I couldn't resolve and unfortunately, a situation that was out of my control. News flash, I'm a control fanatic. I generally don't try to control other people, only situations. Unable to succeed in manipulating a positive outcome in this circumstance, I found I was feeling more and more down. Soon I began to avoid the issue all together and I convinced myself that "fortunately girl you're not living in the dark ages, so move on." And that's exactly what I did, or so I thought.

I had already figured out God's calling for me was taking care of others. I love the Chris Kyle story American Sniper. One of my favorite scenes of all time is when his Dad, while sitting at the dinner table one evening states; "Son, there are wolves, there are sheep, and then there are sheepdogs, be a sheepdog." Of course, Chris grew up, joined the army and became one of the most successful snipers of the war in the middle east. He saved thousands of lives with both his dedication and his accuracy. I knew I was never going to be a Chris Kyle, but I realized that I too could make a difference in my small corner of the world. I am a sheepdog!

CHAPTER 4

THE FAMILY CURSE

Now the true heart of the matter. I'm talking about all the secrets you would want to hide but can't. The ever present "thorn in the side" as the apostle Paul states. Here in this chapter it is revealed.

My mother's side of the family has had a history of clinical depression for generations. Even before the root of such mental illnesses were discovered, folks in poverty in rural Appalachia dealt with the hardships or heartbreak of this unfortunate plight. Our family was no different. Sometimes simply fretting over where our next meal would come from. Is it going to rain, will the garden grow, will I be able to bag a buck when I go out in the morning? Yes, we had all that to worry over, so worry over it we did.

Grandad was notorious for self-medicating, as well as using alcohol. He hoped no one would catch on. He hid it well, because no one really knew except his closest family members. He turned into a completely different person when he had been drinking. The tall lanky man that would laugh and joke constantly, would become unrecognizable after a few drinks. As he grew older, he became frail and unhealthy. My grandmother also had a myriad of health problems. I had decided at that point I would be the one to help take care of the old folks. I thought having no children of my own to tie up a large portion of time, I logistically should be the one to look after my kin. And so, I did.

My grandparents were special people. Grandad had a past and was a bit ornery, but granny had a beautiful soul. I miss them very much still to this day and contribute most of my lifelong lessons to their presence in my young life. "Sally", as my grandad jokingly called me, "Touch that electric fence over there and see if its workin." I loved them so, and I loved my mother who did her best to care for her parents and make them comfortable until their passing in 1996, and in 2010.

My mother has a big heart, and her compassion for others I can only hope to inherit a small portion. She, being a sheepdog herself, cared for several of the little elderly women in our hometown of Alderson, WV. One lady specifically, she grew very close to. Her name was Pearl. She was a dear little retired school-teacher, who was the type that really made you "mind your p's and q's, as my granny would say. Prim and proper, she became a big part of Mom's life. I had moved away to college, then married, and my younger brother grew older and could care for himself. So, momma had Pearl to dote on and foster. We never knew how strong their bond really was until the day momma lost her dear friend. Over time we felt her sadness would wane. She would say, "I spent so much time caring for her in that dark little house, I think I just got depressed."

There it is-that word-depressed. Uughh makes me shudder to this day. I knew momma would overcome, she had before. In fact, nearly everyone in the family had suffered from this debilitating atrocity. "They all survived though right," you ask? Well not exactly. At this point there had been two recorded suicides, a great grandfather and momma's oldest sister Patty. I have only a few, but wonderful memories of Aunt Patty. She had that sweet spirit like her mother, my granny, and was so intelligent. She graduated Valedictorian in high school, received a scholarship, and with honors completed her college career in business and economics. Over time the stress of financial burden, relationship difficulties, and the "ever present" family curse took its toll. One of the saddest times I can remember in our family then ensued. No one could believe that someone so young and vibrant could take their own life. I never knew either until I experienced the darkness for myself. That longing for peace, the sheer hopelessness, leaves you cold and empty. You feel as if you're bringing everyone else down and that they would be better off without you.

Suicide is a tragic circumstance that many are tempted to condemn. It tears apart families and leaves a hole no one else can fill. I imagine it's hard to figure out the reason why someone would even consider taking their own life unless you've walked in their shoes. My lovely aunt and her beautiful soul passed when I was only eight years of age. She left behind two beautiful boys, my first cousins, who are close to my age. Fortunately, after the tragedy they moved in with their father's parents not far from where we lived. I was thrilled we were able to spend our childhood together. We sure had a lot of fun in those days and we are blessed to still enjoy one another's company.

Clinical Depression as defined: feelings of severe sadness and rejection. A mental condition that correlates with a chemical imbalance of norepinephrine and serotonin in the brain. It is characterized by feelings of severe despondency and typically also with feelings of inadequacy and guilt. Major depression is often accompanied by lack of energy and disturbance of appetite and sleep.

I watched helplessly while my mother sank lower into her dark abyss. She rarely spoke and seemed much less interested in what was going on around her. Who is this person, this isn't my Mom? We held family meetings to decide what to do, but we couldn't seem to wrap our brain around a treatment plan involving therapy and possible medication. Was it necessary? Would she agree? We tried several attempts at "cheering her up." Taking her on shopping trips and other excursions only to find her growing irritable and wanting to return home to the safety of the couch. I prayerfully cried out to God to bring my mother back to me, it was she after all who had been with me since the beginning. God's answer came one day unexpectedly. I was standing in my mother's living room, when she made one simple statement; "I do not want to end up like my sister." Sheer panic washed over me, and I knew from that day forward I would find momma the help she needed. I couldn't take that chance, and I was not ready to lose my mother by any means. I found a wonderful psychologist who came highly recommended. Someone who unfortunately, lost her battle with breast cancer, but left a legacy in those she had helped. We also encountered an extremely knowledgeable psychiatrist. One who not only helped Mom obtain a successful medication regimen but became a friend and mentor to us both.

Momma slowly improved over time thanks to the right treatment and proper diagnosis. She still lapses occasionally when things don't seem to be going well. We all do at times. Fortunately, the Lord knew what He was doing when he placed the two of us together. We are one another's support system when those times close in. I encourage her and she encourages me, and together we are overcoming the family curse.

CHAPTER 5

MY TURN

Life goes on, whether we are ready for it or not. I have to say that the next few years had me down on my knees more often than you'd think. Losing the grandparents, both mine and my husbands was traumatic. Considering we both spent a great deal of time with them growing up, life as we knew it would soon have to change. We were so close to that generation and still value their ways of life.

Soon after the grands passed, I almost lost my mother, my guide, to a surgical complication. We lost my young brother-in-law to a car accident after drug involvement. So young and talented, he left us empty and full of regret. A good deal of guilt washed over me during this time, struggling to be there for everyone and trying "to fix" the situations at hand. I couldn't save him, I was powerless. The appointments I had made he wouldn't attend. At times we must learn people have to make their own choices, their own decisions. Losing him made me realize how much we all need God. The Bible says in Psalms 27:14 "Wait on the Lord: be of good courage, and he shall strengthen thine heart: wait, I say, on the Lord." This verse rang true time and time again. Waiting, I must say is not my strong suite. I am a get in there, get it done kind of gal. At this time in life I knew it was pointless for me to do anything but pray. Sometimes you must give up that control, the kind you never truly have in the first place. I'm not the great physician, able to heal others in an instant. I am nothing compared to an Almighty God who is more than capable of creating this world and everything in it. After all He is the Father of our very existence, turn everything over to God.

Jeremiah 29:11; For I know the thoughts that I think toward you, saith the Lord, thoughts of peace, and not of evil, to give you and expected end.

That is a special verse to me and deserves its own space. It hangs on my wall to this day. Simply put, God provides for us throughout our lifetime, both during the good times and the bad. Hills and valleys, He is always there. He healed my mother and for that I am forever grateful. My brother in law, the little guy I had known since the age of three, unfortunately lost his life. I had literally only felt the actual physical pain from a heartbreak when I lost my favorite uncle. Those military funerals still get me, I loved that man so much. Little brother, however, was so young and so full of potential that his death brought feelings that are difficult to describe. I'm convinced that giving the pain and hurt over to God is the only way to overcome grief. He covers it all. "Casting all your care upon him; for He careth for you." (1 Peter 5:7.)

So, you ask, "is this where the rubber meets the road?" "Is this where you had a meltdown?" No, in fact the meltdown came later. I'm convinced God carried me through these hard times, kept me mentally strong so that I could be there for others. It was when I stopped looking to Him and depending on His will in my life, that's where I ran into trouble. Trust me, Baptist guilt can be a good thing. God sends these storms to impress upon His children that they are headed down a dark and sinful path.

I clearly remember a time sitting in my truck in the new and husband approved garage we had just built, thinking hey I've really done well. I drove to work feeling proud of myself, not thinking of the real reason I had been so blessed. I work hard, after all, I deserve nice things. We don't have children to save for, so we can afford to spend on things that make us happy as a couple. "Stupid girl," looking back that was the beginning of your chastisement. "What you did, really?" "It's not what you have done, it's what God has done." So, I sank deeper and deeper into the delusion that material things matter. New truck, new tack for the horses, sprucing up the house, working overtime to pay it off. I never liked debt. My focus became what I could somehow acquire and not the things that really mattered. The important things were my family, my friends, my coworkers, their lives and what they needed. My church and my church family, all seemed to "play second fiddle." Yes, I still attended church, still taught Sunday School, but for the first time in my life, I kept God at a distance. I failed to communicate with Him as I once did. My prayer life suffered. I didn't spend time in His word like I should. The ways of the world had caught up to me. I wanted more "stuff."

"Pride goeth before destruction, and an haughty spirit before a fall." Proverbs 16:18

CHAPTER 6

THE MELTDOWN

I started having small periods of anxiety in January of 2007. Nothing major, just periodically throughout the day I began experiencing a "gnawing" feeling in my gut. I shrugged it off as having SAD or Seasonal Affective Disorder. Mid-Winter, more darkness, cold weather, is not conducive for a country girl who loves the outdoors and sunshine. "This too shall pass," my friends would tell me. So, I convinced myself when Spring came it would. But I was wrong.

Do you remember early on when I said I loved my animals as if they were my children? Well I'm still guilty of this at times, I know most of us animal lovers are. I felt this way toward my two Labrador retrievers. I had a Yellow female I dearly loved, Maggie. I had purchased her in Colorado and brought her back East with me. She was such a sweet even-tempered little lady, not to mention beautiful, so I decided to breed her. She had a boisterous litter of chocolates and blacks, but then developed seizures sometime after their birth. After vetting her for those, I decided not to breed again and had her spayed. I kept the runt of the litter a little black male we named Bandit. I later changed his name to Bubba, because believe me it was well suited for the little mischief maker. He was obsessed with balls and playing fetch. One Summer I discovered my green tomatoes were disappearing from the garden. "Pesky deer," you might ask? No, it was my Bubba thinking he had found these wonderful green balls that would magically appear out of nowhere on little green vines. I had many backyard adventures with these two. We went wading in the river and enjoyed cruising the backroads with their ears flapping in the breeze. My momma even went as far to say those dogs are "her best friends." Looking back, I suppose they were.

What does this canine kinship have to do with a mental break? Seems totally unrelated, right? Animals are supposed to bring us joy, provide companionship, become an armchair therapist. All of this is true, no doubt, and maybe, just maybe these reasons are why we take their death so personally. That Summer Maggie at age 15, could no longer walk. She was failing, her organs were shutting down, I knew it was time. Unfortunately, Bubba two years her junior, was diagnosed with a large cell tumor. Thinking I could end both their suffering in one fail swoop, I asked my veterinarian at the time to end the lives of my good friends. He was kind and obliged performing the grueling task in the bed of our truck with just he, his assistant, my husband, and I. Once again, I felt the heartbreak, somehow it seemed to cut deeply this time. I had other animals to care for, so I forged ahead. My family and close friends knew my sadness and did their best to console me. Still others I knew just shook their heads, "they're just animals," they would say. I have always hated that statement.

So, the change happened after that day. Even though more subtle then I can remember I'm sure, the darkness seemed to hit me "like a ton of bricks." One morning soon after my loss, I went to work. In going through my normal routine, I immediately felt like I was having difficulty even putting one foot in front of the other. I was down, it was over. Those little periods of anxiety had built over time, and my dogs, my friends were my trigger.

For me there has always been a trigger. By trigger I mean something that sparks my depression. Generally, if I'm worrying about something or someone over an extended length of time then that's my pitfall. People I care about, my animals, or once again that ugly obsession with money hoarding is at the top of the list. Thinking back, I knew I had been under stress, fretting over how to pay for all the home improvements. Granted some of them were needed, and some were elective, I began thinking we had "bit off more that we could chew." Suddenly, as with many depressed folks, reality started becoming a little hazy. Molehills were becoming mountains. I've never liked drama, or wanted anything associated with it, but at this point I was becoming quite the drama queen.

I can remember losing site of a few entries in my checkbook, thanks to the introduction of the debit card. Yes, I'm old and I was around when they invented this version of plastic. I flew into a panic, stopping by the bank checking with my dear "bank lady," wondering how I had gotten to this point. I wasn't bankrupt mind you, not even close. But the thought of having less money than I realized was a good dose of saying "wake up girl, you just ain't right." She seemed to sense my plight and when I went to leave that evening, she hugged me and said, "I'll be praying for you". I came home crying hysterically. So much so it worried my husband and my parents. Even though I couldn't acknowledge just what my issues were, they could see me struggling. My Dad even came that evening to help me balance my checkbook and assist with budget and finance planning. I'm usually very good at managing money, my parents taught me well. At that point, however, my state of mind had me convinced I had lost control of just about everything. My confidence was waning, I was fearful of becoming totally incompetent and basically failing miserably. My husband and his Dad were out fixing my pasture fence after a post meets water line incident, and I remember thinking "I'm too much trouble, my horses are too much trouble, everything I have going on right now is too much trouble." This is ridiculous I thought, I've always been independent, why do I suddenly need everyone in my life to come to my rescue. What is wrong with me? My husband kept telling me over and over "snap out of it, you're stronger than this." He's right, right? I am strong. I am a strong and independent woman. I realized, of course, this was wrong on so many levels! My strength comes from above, not from within, or had I forgotten that?

I continued my downward spiral and darkness seemed to consume me. I had a sick horse, at that time too. My gelding was experiencing lameness issues. I don't mean to dwell on this topic but trust me dwelling was something I became very well versed at. I repeatedly experienced the guilt and regret that I had allowed him to consume too much pasture. In turn this can lead to the dreaded illness, laminitis or founder. In horses it can be a death sentence. A word to the wise, chubby little quarter horses who constantly have their head to the ground, should not be allowed to free roam. That soon became my focus.

As in many depressed people there is always something to occupy that troubled mind. I would imagine the worst, live out the possible scenarios, and ponder the "what-ifs." Sound familiar? If you have lived to experience depression you understand. You contemplate the worst possible things that could happen in order to not be so surprised and mortified when they do. So, do they happen? Sometimes and sometimes not. The point of all this worry, I'm convinced is a means of self-punishment. I felt guilty for losing my grip on reality and for allowing bad things to happen to my fur babies. In that state of mind, you are constantly in utter misery. A "depressed person" is a "distressed person."

Unfortunately, I could find no relief at that point. I cried daily.

I cried to my husband and he would try to comfort me, but to no avail I couldn't be comforted. I would call my mother and just cry. Always it was about the horse, the regret of the pain I seen him go through. I failed at my horsemanship which in translation meant I failed as a mother. Momma knew all along that this wasn't normal behavior and tried to convince me. "Where's my girl, where's that smile? It's gone for now, but I know it will be back." She'd say honey," I know you this is not just about the horse." "There is something wrong, you need help." "I'll be fine" I said, "once I can get my horse better."

CHAPTER 7

DENIAL

Denial: as defined by asserting that a statement or allegation is not true. That's where I was, denial. Surely, I'm stronger than that, I'm not going to fall prey to the family curse. I know better because I'm a healthcare professional. I can handle most anything, or so I thought. Meanwhile, my friends and my co-workers began to take notice. They could see the path I was headed and tried to leave subtle messages letting me know I really needed help. Looking back, I know it seemed childish for a woman in her mid to late thirties to be pining over a horse, and to be mourning dogs. That's something that a little girl seven or eight years old would do. That's part of the depression you know, you find yourself regressing to a much simpler time in your life. At least that's how I responded. I remember thinking I don't want to feel this way, I'm losing myself.

Other members of my family began to take notice. A dear aunt and uncle noticed just by the sadness on my face. They checked on me often and even took me out on the lake in their boat. Knowing I love the water and fishing is a favorite pastime, they hoped to cheer me and take my mind off the hurt. My mother in law would check on me often, and seeing the exhaustion and angst in my eyes she would ask, "Roberta, are you sick?" Still I refused to get help.

I even spoke with family members over the phone, telling them I don't need medication, I have God. I wholeheartedly believed that God could and would help me through the mental anguish. I learned then and there what it means to fall prostate before God. Face down on the bathroom floor multiple times a week, I would cry and beg for God to take away the darkness. I'd say" Lord, I'm a broken vessel." "I can't be an effective servant towards you, unless you repair all the cracks, and fill me again." Little did I realize this was God's way of molding and shaping me. He's the potter, I am the clay. Do you remember me saying, "I was getting too big for my britches," and that God's ways are higher than our ways? Unfortunately, it took months before this epiphany would come to me.

"To add fuel to the fire" so to speak, thanks to the constant anxiety, insomnia struck. I found myself going multiple nights at a time without sleep. In fact, I was taking rather large doses of Benadryl, in order to fall asleep. It didn't keep me asleep, however, and I would wake up at 3 or 3:30am my mind racing with "what ifs." Depression will do that, destroy your sleeping habits. You either don't sleep enough or you sleep too much. Your appetite wanes or increases. I looked like the "walking dead." I couldn't eat, I couldn't sleep, I lost weight, I looked frail and was utterly exhausted. My work suffered and I just couldn't focus. I felt guilt towards my co-workers. They were depending on me to be their leader and I felt I was failing them. Instead I found I was working hard at getting out of work. I was fearful that in my state of mind I would make a mistake.

Finally, a wonderful mentor of mine, former nurse leader pulled me aside. "Honey," she said, "are you trying to lose weight." I answered "no," and dropped my head. My secret was out, I couldn't deny what they were all seeing. Once a normally chipper, hardworking gal, was turning into a shadow of her former self right in front of their eyes. She encouraged me to seek counseling, and to accept the fact that taking medication "will sometimes get you over the hump." I continued to deny the need for such treatment. After all stubbornness runs in the family too. In my mind getting counseling and especially taking meds would be against the law of God. After all He was all needed, He would see me through. No doubt in my mind He did, but not yet.

The day came when I took my horse to a nearby veterinary center, where they along with an awesome farrier helped me get him back on track. The vet assured me I would be riding him again by that Spring. So, I thought life is good again, things are getting better. Did they? No, I found something else to worry over. I don't even remember now what the "something else" was. All I know is that the sleepless nights, the incessant worry, and now a huge weight of guilt had overcome me. I can vaguely remember finding my mother bathing her Pug one Saturday afternoon. Overcome with the misery, I collapsed at her feet, telling her "Mom, I can't do this anymore." She and my Dad, took me by the hand, sit me down, and said "girl it's time for you to get help."

Why had I fought against the help I needed for so long? I knew the resources, after all I had utilized them in the past with Mom. I'm in healthcare, I had seen textbook cases of depression and other mental illnesses. I knew the score of how it ran in our family, and the tragedies that had resulted because of it. Mom made the appointment, then took me still "kicking and screaming" to my first counseling session. She had discussed with my counselor prior to my arrival on how everyone thought that this "breakdown" was over the fact that I would never have children. I however, still thought it was over finances, dogs, and a horse. So, we preceded in delving deep into my psyche to find the problem. At first, I was against this, I didn't want to be mentally probed. It was pride that kept me from admitting anything was significantly wrong. I was in a funk and I would snap out of it. It was just taking longer this time. Too long.

CHAPTER 8

IN THE THROWS

For those of you who are questioning as I did if you are experiencing clinical depression, here's how to know for certain. I want to add a list of symptoms, not to convince you, but so that you yourself can see if it's really happening. To diagnose clinical depression, many doctors use the symptom criteria for major depressive disorder in the Diagnostic and Statistical Manual of Mental Disorders (DSM-5), published by the American Psychiatric Association. Signs and symptoms of clinical depression may include:

Feelings of sadness, tearfulness, emptiness, or hopelessness

Angry outbursts, irritability or frustration, even over small matters

Loss of interest or pleasure in most or all normal activities

Sleep disturbances, including insomnia or sleeping too much

Tiredness and lack of energy, so even small tasks take extra effort

Reduced appetite and weight loss or increased cravings for food and weight gain

Anxiety, agitation or restlessness

Slowed thinking, speaking or body movements

Feelings of worthlessness or guilt, fixating on past failures or self-blame

Trouble thinking, concentrating, making decisions and remembering things

Frequent or recurrent thoughts, suicide attempts or suicide

Unexplained physical problems

Any of these symptoms are usually severe enough to cause noticeable problems in relationships with others, or in day-to-day activities. Now I'm just an old surgical nurse here, but if you as the reader experience any or all these symptoms as I did, please seek help. I would be failing at my intent of bringing to attention the seriousness of an illness most want to keep hidden. What keeps us from the help we need? Pride, guilt, shame, any number of things. It was all of these and more for me. My reasoning for neglecting my need for treatment had a good deal to do with being raised in the Baptist faith. I know this sounds contradictory, but the heart of the matter is most pastors, deacons, teachers in the Baptist church preach and teach against mental health treatment. Especially the use of medications, and I was no different. Why on earth would I need mind-altering drugs when I have in my heart my Lord and Savior Jesus Christ? Believe me I value my Christian roots, and I am by no means placing blame on anyone or on any defined doctrine. I'm sure Baptists are not an isolated group, when it comes to these thoughts and opinions on depression. Truth be told, the title of this book came from a Catholic friend of mine. A fellow nurse, she is a dear sweet soul and has been one of my very good friends throughout the years. Every time she would share a guilty profession, she would claim "it's that Catholic guilt." I would laugh and say, "Baptists are the same, it must be universal."

We are pressed upon from the beginning, sin will lead to an ultimate downfall. As my little gray-haired Sunday school teacher used to say; "sin will take you farther than you want to go." That statement is true and there is no doubt that sin is an ongoing factor in our separation from God. The key is to openly confess, and God will always deliver redemption. If we humble ourselves, not be stubborn or willful, and confess the wrongdoing, he will draw us out of the miry pit of sin. However, that's not to say He doesn't sometimes allow those walls or beliefs we once held true to be broken down. As these walls crumble, it will in turn reveal to us a better way. His way. Thus, setting us on a path of purpose living in His will and His alone. I love my church and my church family, and by far being Baptist is an essential part of life for me. I feel as if God wants me to share this testimony of mine to allow fellow believers of all faiths to seek the help they need, without the stigma attached. God does heal and sustain the troubled mind. I need for those of you who may doubt to realize He sometimes works through others. For example, counselors, spiritual leaders, and fellow believers. That's their calling, be thankful for them and let them fulfill God's will for their life.

Our Bible tells us of God-fearing men who suffered mentally. "A man after God's own heart," King David spent many agonizing nights mourning over his sin and the effect it had on the life of his children. Even before his guilty plot of adultery and murder, David ran from King Saul. Saul was constantly trying to kill David, his future replacement. Poor David was hiding in caves and secret places, wondering if he would even survive the next twenty-four hours. If that doesn't cause mental trauma, I don't know what does. He sometimes found himself in great distress and would cry out to God for relief. Sounds familiar, huh? I would tell myself, "you know, I have no real reason for these feelings. I really haven't had a traumatic event in my life." Yes, I've had some hard times but nothing to warrant a mental break. Not like King David, who spoke in 2 Samuel chapter 22 verses 2-7; "And he said, The Lord is my rock, and my fortress, and my deliverer; The God of my rock; in him will I trust: he is my shield, and the horn of my salvation, my high tower, and my refuge, my savior; thou savest me from violence. I will call on the Lord, who is worthy to be praised: so shall I be saved from mine enemies. When the waves of death compassed me, the floods of ungodly men made me afraid; The sorrows of hell compassed me about; the snares of death prevented me; In my distress I called upon the Lord, and cried to my God; and he did hear my voice out of his temple, and my cry did enter his ears."

David's close relationship with God allowed him to not only escape the snares of Saul, but to find repentance and remittance from sin. I experienced nothing of the sort, I wasn't running in fear for my life. I began to add layer after layer of guilt, simply because I found no real reason for my despair. I would ask myself, "how can I as a Christian, who has that hope and that promise of heaven, be experiencing such mental pain?" I'm getting to that.

I think it's a safe bet that King David didn't have Xanax or Prozac or any of the multiple med choices we have today. Would he have taken them if he could? They would not only relieve the distress, but to help him stay focused on his God and his kingdom? If he would have known how these meds would improve his condition, would he have accepted treatment? Doubtful, statistics claim men are even less likely than women to seek help.

I have often thought of the apostle Paul as well, throughout his crusade. His proverbial "thorn in the flesh." What was that all about? Bible scholars have pondered this question for centuries. To my knowledge people have speculated, but really have no idea what the issue was that plagued Paul. Some say poor eyesight, others suspect malaria, or even epilepsy. While an actual physical diagnosis seems likely, has anyone ever considered that he may have been depressed? After all, it was Paul who before his encounter with Christ on the road to Damascus, organized massacres against new Christians. Wouldn't that be a gigantic source of guilt, shame and reproach. We may never know what "the thorn" may have been, that is until we reach heaven. Rest assured Paul knew, and he also knew that this sickness, infirmity, or condition was God's way of keeping him in check. Paul stated in 2 Corinthians 12:7; "And lest I should be exalted above measure through the abundance of the revelations, there was given to me a thorn in the flesh, the messenger of Satan to buffet me, lest I should be exalted above measure." Wait, hold on a second. Wasn't that what I was doing months earlier, wasn't I feeling proud and exalting my own self. What if this depression is God's way of reeling me in? If so, it is painful, "please God make it stop, I get it."

CHAPTER 9

DIAGNOSIS PLEASE!

Suffice it to say that up to this point I had gotten no relief. All the prayers I knew that God was hearing, but having to wait on the answer, it was just plain rough. I had been to several counseling sessions, as a matter of fact I began to crave them. The reason for the faithful attendance to all those sessions, the ones I was reluctant to participate in at first, was less than obvious. Every appointment I anxiously drove too, I suppose gave me new hope as to finding a cure for this wretched darkness. Imagine being in a deep, dark pit, walls covered in slimy mud, two cinderblocks chained to both ankles, trying to claw your way out. Okay that was a little dramatic, but trust me, that's how it felt. The light at the end of the tunnel wasn't anywhere in sight.

To make matters worse it was Summertime, my favorite time of year. My husband, as well, as the rest of my family thought things would be on the up and up for me. Mainly my mood. Unfortunately, it was during the time period that my father in law was diagnosed with a terminal illness. He was a trooper and fought it for several years before his death. I thought this is the kick in the pants that I need and to focus on someone other than myself. I quickly went to work finding the right treatment plan for him with the help of surgeons I knew from my unit. For a while I was able to occupy myself with getting the help he needed and push aside that dreadful feeling. It soon returned with a vengeance, however, along with all the symptoms. "I have to fight this," I would tell myself "people need me." I tried, and I'd like to say I succeeded, but my mind was still weighed down by the anxiousness and worry. I had just found one more thing to worry over. Pray, I'd tell myself, pray like you've never prayed before. I would for him, and then I would quickly plead for God to remove this mental block. I needed it gone in order to be an effective servant. "What was the holdup God?" Soon I'll learn.

As Fall arrived in the mountains and the leaves were turning, I was getting worse. My therapist had finally decided to have me take one of the psychological diagnostic tests which quickly revealed that I truly was clinically depressed. She said, "It says here you feel guilt at an alarming sense, what do you have to feel guilty over," I muttered something through the tears about the horse, about not being a good person lately because of these feelings, and I rushed out of the office. There it was my diagnosis, and I couldn't deny it anymore. I drove to my mother's house as I had so many times before. I declared to her that "I have it too," the family curse. We cried, I asked my stepfather to pray, we prayed. Then my momma said, "girl you know what you have to do."

So, I consented to having my counselor set up an appointment with a local psychiatrist. Here was the lady I knew had helped my mom. I was still reluctant, however, when the medication was offered. I don't think I need that, I have God, I have prayer and reading His word. Medication to me would mean I was failing as a Christian, right? Multiple people encouraged me to try the meds, stating that it would help me out of the slump faster. In turn, going without it could possibly take months to even years in overcoming the affliction. Still other folks would say, "no you don't need drugs, they'll just turn you into a zombie, make you numb."

Shameful as it was to me, I finally consented to trying a small dose. I just couldn't withstand the mental torment any longer. My wake-up call finally came the day my mother stated that I reminded her so much of her sister. "What, the sister who committed suicide?" Merciful heavens, that can't be. I had never contemplated suicide up to that point and didn't plan on making that an option. I was spooked, I had to do something. So, I began to ignore the naysayers and opted for chemical relief. Determined not to become dependent, my wonderful physician began a light regimen. It's common to have to tweak or trial other classes of drugs in order to find what works. Fortunately for me doc's recommendation began to work immediately. There were times I had setbacks, irritability, mood swings, but overall saw improvement for the next few months. I had discussed my concerns with my psychiatrist. Priority one: My faith in God; the Bible states in a favorite verse of mine "Be careful for nothing; but in every thing by prayer and supplication with thanksgiving let your requests be made known unto God." (Philippians 4:6) Will my fellow believers look down on me, because I relented or "failed" so to speak to allow God to heal my mental plight? Priority two: I've been in healthcare along time, I know how cynical we all become. We all witness constant addiction and turmoil from the use of similar drugs. How will my coworkers and those in other departments feel about me being a leader? Will they think I can't handle the responsibility? Priority three: My family, they're Christians too. Will I be a complete and utter disappointment?

All those reasons I just mentioned seem selfish, don't they? It seems as if I was more worried how I would look or how their reactions would make me feel. What about God? Where did He fit in? Turns out He was there all along. (Hebrews 13:5) "I will never leave thee, nor forsake thee." I'll reveal in the final chapter what I learned from this entire ordeal. Lessons from God are life's greatest blessings. This idea is hard to imagine when you're living them, but truly they are by His design. "What doesn't kill you makes you stronger," and last I checked I wasn't a zombie.

CHAPTER 10

REVIVAL

"Anxiety is sin." Believe it or not I have heard this in a sermon recently from a visiting minister. It's disheartening and not entirely true. How can we as Christians get so caught up in a world that only creates strife and brings us turmoil? As I stated before, sometimes there are other reasons besides grief and long-term sadness that causes the downward spiral. Genetics, trauma, real reasons that set us apart. Sometimes I feel as there are outside forces that manage to deter our good works or cause a Christian to stumble. Namely, the old devil. You honestly didn't think I could write my testimony without mentioning him, did you? He is the author of confusion, contempt, and just plain old wickedness. "Be sober, be vigilant; because your adversary the devil, as a roaring lion walketh about, seeking whom he may devour;" 1 Peter 5:8. The trick is to realize, and God will help you do this, when Satan is trying to "pull the wool over your eyes". He can make something seemingly innocent become a crushing blow to the testimony of an otherwise faithful servant of God. There is no doubt, Satan had a hand in causing my life's current disruption. After all, I fell prey to the old ploy of wanting what my neighbors had and lifting myself up, when I know that only God is in charge. I had no control of my own even though I liked to think I did. I tell my Sunday school kids this all the time. God will not separate Himself from you, but you can separate yourself from Him. How you might ask? My Sunday school kids know the answer, by sinning. Sin causes God to grieve, and more importantly being the holy heavenly Father, God cannot look upon sin. When Jesus died for us on the cross, the saddest moment I'm certain for Him, was being separated from His father God. Jesus was perfect and holy, but at that moment he bore our sin. Mark 15:34 "And at the ninth hour Jesus cried with a loud voice, saying, Eloi, Eloi, lama sabachthani? Which is, being interpreted, My God, my God, why hast thou forsaken me? Separation from God is painful, and this is a lesson I learned very well.

Further discussion with my doctor led to some sensible solutions for my plan of treatment. Getting over the guilt of failing God, my family, my church, my coworkers, my animals, was not at the heart of my problem. I neglected the simple fact that depression and anxiety can be caused by a medical condition and/or genetic tendency. The brain is a complex organ, according to my doctor, an unexplored universe. We know the ins and outs of the kidneys, the heart, the large intestine, but the brain in many ways remains a mystery. Sort of the outer space region of the body, a vast unknown. Yes, there are those chemical imbalances, working both inside and outside the nerve cells. Probable causes can also be faulty mood regulation by the brain, genetic tendencies, stressful life events, medications, and medical problems, to name a few. Then she spoke the statement that finally made me feel a bit better. "You're a nurse, if you had high blood pressure, you would treat it right?" "If you had diabetes, you would treat that." It made so much sense to me. Medication for brain abnormalities? That was a new spin. I think it appealed to the healthcare side of me. Is medication socially acceptable though for a Christian? Will it harm my testimony? I really have no real reason to be so anxious, life has not dealt me an overly cruel hand. A barrage of questions filled my lips. My Baptist family won't see it as a medical condition, they'll see it as a failure on my part. Anxiety is sin. Taking mind altering drugs is sin. Then she spoke another wise statement. "Tell that to a young girl who was molested as a child." "Tell the young women who was beaten and abandoned by her partner." "Tell them there is no good reason for their anxiety, for their panic attacks." "Tell them there is no good reason, for needing help in order to overcome those horrific events." I sobbed bitterly after hearing this and prayed. "Lord please help those who are suffering from the darkness, no matter the cause."

CHAPTER 11

ON THE MEND

Knowing now what I didn't know then helps make me more aware of how grateful and thankful I am to have had a blessed childhood. There are those like my doctor mentioned in the previous chapter who were not so fortunate. If anyone has a reason for anxiety and need for treatment, it would be those dear people. I've known young girls in my youth group who because of drug ridden mothers, and absent father figures, have practically had to raise themselves. I love those girls. For me seeing their strong bond and caring for one another, helped me understand that life isn't always about circumstances or things. It's about the people by your side. Others matter. I've forged many great friendships as a result of this realization. Wonderful friends. Friends that will stick by you through "thick and thin." One more reason to praise God for the difficult times. It is then when He reveals to you that the important things in life are not necessarily things.

Even though I knew my anxiety and depression was not a result of some traumatic event or stressful atrocity, I knew there had to be a reason. Genetics. My mother's grandfather had committed suicide by hanging himself from the barn rafters. Riddled with anxiety my own grandfather, my mother's father, was an alcoholic in the early years and later ate Valium like candy. My momma and her siblings "grew up hard" because of this. Aunts, uncles, cousins have all had their experience with a case of the "Family nerves." It isn't something to take lightly. We have all chosen to suppress those feelings at some point in our lives, but unfortunately repression is not a healthy means of coping. I want to encourage each of my family members who may be dealing with this disorder to seek help. It's not our fault, it's an inherited condition. Please don't refrain from treatment based on what others may think. Life is just too short to live in "mental misery."

Slowly, I began to find my way out of the darkness. I think looking back at my heritage, ugly truths and all, helped me to feel a little less guilt. Still, I knew that God was revealing to me things that I needed to do. Trial by fire, I had always heard. Maybe these dark times are here not so much to punish, but to force me to bend. I had always been one to set limits on God. "Yes, God I'll do that mission trip, but now is not the time." "I'm too busy, my work schedule is too hectic right now." "Yes, I need to witness more, but the people here are just not receptive." Excuses, excuses. Time and time again I have quenched the Holy Spirit, in times when I should have opened my heart and mind. Let's face it, we're all guilty of this shortcoming. And nothing works faster than God getting your attention through a serious struggle.

After months on end of walking in darkness, I hardly recognized my former self. Gradually, the light began to show through the cracks of my tattered soul and slowly I began to feel better. My focus became clearer and I began to enjoy the little things again. Going through the depression the things I loved had become a burden. My horses had become a burden. The care, the feeding, all those things I had found therapeutic before, now just monotony. I had been going through the motions so to speak. Mucking stalls, brushing manes and tails, and listening to the sound of the animals happily munching their grain, would be the perfect ending to an otherwise ordinary day. Gradually those warm fuzzy feelings started coming back. God had allowed my battle-scarred psyche to return to some form of my previous self, tired, weary, but wise.

Beloved, think it not strange concerning the fiery trial which is to try you, as though some strange thing happened unto you: But rejoice, inasmuch as ye are partakers of Christ's sufferings; that, when his glory shall be revealed, ye may be glad also with exceeding joy. (1 Peter 4:12-13)

CHAPTER 12

STILL SMALL VOICE

I spoke of David and his plight in an earlier chapter and how he became discouraged being hunted by Saul. The anxiety, stress, and unconfessed sin almost destroyed him and members of his own family. There are many other examples of great men and women of God who at sundry times began to feel downtrodden. Perhaps the one that had the most impact on me is a beloved Old Testament prophet. Someone whom I wholeheartedly believe experienced the weight of depression. Elijah the faithful man of God. The poor fella was on the run like David. The evil queen Jezebel was gunning for him because Elijah had rid the world from the cruel priests of the false god Baal. In 1 Kings chapter 19 we hear the story of how God had proven multiple times He would never leave Elijah. He sent an angel to comfort, feed and encourage the prophet. God then sent Elijah on a long journey where he came to a cave. The cave had been prepared by God to be a haven for the prophet. Instead, Elijah decided it would be a good venue for him to throw his own pity party. It was there God confronted Elijah about his feelings and his faith. The Almighty God already knew Elijah's problem was depression and discouragement. God also knew that these feelings would render this prophet unable to effectively share His message to the people of Israel. This opportunity however, allowed Elijah to acknowledge and reveal for himself the truth of the matter. It's important as Christians to pray and speak to God, so that He can help us discover things about ourselves. It may perhaps be the thoughts we've held in secret, or those we are in denial of. I love this passage of scripture where God exerts His power and might in order to convince Elijah not to feel sorry for himself, but to overcome the affliction. I cannot do the passage justice unless I present it as it was inspired by the Lord Himself.

"And he said, Go forth, and stand upon the mount before the Lord. And, behold, the Lord passed by, and a great and strong wind rent the mountains, and brake in pieces the rocks before the Lord; but the Lord was not in the wind; and after the wind an earthquake; but the Lord was not in the earthquake: And after the earthquake a fire; but the Lord was not in the fire: and after the fire a still small voice."

Isn't it wonderful to know an Almighty God who can do so many powerful acts, and yet respond ever so gently to our frail human spirit? That still small voice became a beacon for Elijah. The man of God had become fearful of the one thing so many of us face. The feeling of being alone. Christians need never fear desertion for God is always there. However, most of us desire the presence of others and even need to depend on others in order to cope with their daily lives. We, being human, depend on sight and substance in order to believe. Hebrews 11:1 tells us "Now faith is the substance of things hoped for, the evidence of things not seen." Elijah couldn't see the seven thousand in Israel, "the ones whose knees have not bowed unto Baal," but the reassurance of God's still small voice gave him the faith he needed. That whisper gave him the courage to leave the darkness of that cavern and come down from the mountain. God's hope for Elijah was to further his ministry and turn God's wayward people back to Him.

I make this point because while going through my darkest times, I couldn't seem to gain comfort from the ones I loved. The only comfort I seemed to receive came from God through prayer and the reading of His word. Folks, that takes faith. The inability to see God, coupled with the fear in knowing something is not quite right mentally can be overwhelming. When that feeling comes look to His word. Find those stories of Elijah, David, Paul, and many others and use them as a springboard to empower your personal relationship with the Father. He will send the comforter, the Holy Spirit. Speaking from experience believe me you don't have to be a mighty prophet for that "still small voice" to be heard.

We in turn, as fellow believers, should use our still small voice in comforting others who may be going through similar trials of guilt and depression. You can usually tell when someone is experiencing the tribulation of a mental health disorder. The screening tool I presented earlier is usually very visible to those who know the person well. I've often found myself observing their actions, and sometimes the look on their face can be their tell-tale sign. When I see the hurt and the pain, I generally can't help but confront them about it, knowing that I may be the only one who does. I'll sometimes say, "I know that face, you want to know how, because I've seen that face before staring back at me in the mirror." I then break into conversation, share my testimony, and reassure them that they are not alone in their struggles. Most of us experiencing the doubts, the fears, and the what-ifs, seem to find affirmation in the similar experiences of others. It also can be frustrating on the flip side trying to convince those who have never been saddled with the sadness on how it can bring you down so low. It almost seems that they feel we should all have an internal switch that we can flip on and off in order to control moments of distress. I would be the first in line for one of those believe me. Trust me when I say it's not something that we can shut down automatically. It lingers, it lurks around corners, and just when you think you see a glimmer of light, it clouds the way. I don't know how many times I heard "snap out of it", "pull yourself up by your bootstraps", and "Cheer up, things will get better." We absolutely know your intentions are good, but in our state of mind it feels belittling and derogatory. I finally got downright ugly with my spouse one day because he kept saying "You Need to Chill Out." I eventually apologized, and then the poor guy asked, "What should I say?" I then replied how about "I'm here for ya babe," "I'm praying for you", or "how can I help?" Again, I say a "still small voice" will take you so much farther in effectively communicating with someone dealing with the angst and despair of depression.

CHAPTER 13

OPPORTUNITY KNOCKS

After months on end, my dark cloud started to give way and the sun began to shine once more. I was elated. I praised God knowing that I could once again be an effective servant. Turns out, I realized the pain and the darkness taught me to bend and even break, allowing me to be even more useful as an instrument for God. I cried here I am God, I'm an empty vessel, fill me and use me as you will. I stopped limiting God. I came to Him more humbly, with prayer and supplication." God I'm ready," I said. Immediately, the opportunities began to flow and so did the blessings.

One Sunday afternoon at our annual church hayride and picnic two of the older girls I had taught in Sunday School, came to me with a proposal. "Miss Roberta, would you consider being our new youth leader?" Our little country church had been without a youth leader for several months. "Absolutely", I said. After all, how can I turn down such a request? These young girls desired the word of God, and seemingly God chose me to be their messenger. So, our little group grew and soon my Sunday nights were filled with good times, laughter, and learning about God. As well as food, don't forget the food, after all we are Baptists. We focused on Jesus, His teachings, and how He came to earth to seek and to save. We tackled tough issues facing teens, the usual temptations such as drugs, alcohol, and relationships.

Somehow in our time that we shared, rising tensions grew amongst members. Two very different groups emerged from our little flock. It almost seemed as though some division was taking place; those kids that were raised in church, and those whose parents had never brought them to church. There were different views about worldly topics and dealing with situations as newborn Christians. I knew in my heart we had to find common ground. We fostered role playing, put yourself in another's shoes type of learning methods. I wanted my church raised crew to realize that some of these outside teens had grown up with abusive, neglectful, and oftentimes absent parents. I reminded the church fostered group that they had been fortunate enough to have been blessed with parents who were nurturing. They had parents who took the time to teach them about our loving God. Passing judgement, you see, breeds hatred and harbors a world of resentment. You not only hurt the person you judge, you hurt yourself. Judgement is sin, and though we don't uphold the things that are sinful, we are to love that person and share with them the gospel. Remember sin separates us from a holy God.

What we need to remember is living outside His will only breeds misery and strife. If they could only learn one thing in this class, I wanted them to learn Christ taught forgiveness and mercy to all. Who are we to judge one another? God's word states "Judge not, and ye shall not be judged: condemn not, and ye shall not be condemned: forgive, and ye shall be forgiven: (Luke 6:37). This is the precious words of Jesus. Luke chapter six further depicts the Savior's word of warning. Verses forty and forty-one say "The disciple is not above his master: but every one that is perfect shall be as his master. And why beholdest thou the mote that is in thy brother's eye, but perceives not the beam that is in thine own eye?" Remember as kids we were taught that it was improper to point your finger at someone, and that you had four more fingers pointing back at you. That's what Jesus is saying in this passage. "Judge not, that ye be not judged." (Matthew 7:1) Plain and simple. Leave the judgement to the Father, we are no less guilty than the worst of sinners. Romans 14:13 tells us "Let us not therefore judge one another any more: but judge this rather, that no man put a stumblingblock or an occasions to fall in his brother's way." In other words, we are not to judge anyone but ourselves, for certainly passing judgement may hinder another Christian to grow in their faith. It can also turn away an unbeliever and be considered hypocritical. Oh Boy, there's a word I despise, hypocrisy. By all means, stand up for what you believe, but guard yourselves in order not to offend. Sometimes it can be a fine line.

Also, a good example of a stumbling block came from this very same group of youngsters. After our lesson I would allow fifteen or twenty minutes of recreation which often occurred in our church's basement. It was uniquely built for our youth and Awana programs, as it housed several games and a rather large room for play. The kids loved to play dodgeball, and I myself even joined in. Fun times, right? Well so we thought. One night two of the older boys began arguing over who was out and who wasn't. Their words soon turned into let's see who can hit who the hardest. Before I could deescalate, a curse word flew from the mouth of one of my oldest and most faithful members. Everyone gasped and looked at him, then looked at me. I said, "young man you go right now and tell your mother what you just said." A few minutes later his mother came down from the church sanctuary and asked if she could talk to me. I obliged, and we walked outside the classroom. She then stated "Roberta, I have never approved of this game within the church walls, it seems to only breed violence and arguments amongst the kids." At that moment I knew it would be the end of our dodgeball games. What seemed like an innocent form of exercise had become offensive to a fellow believer. I could no longer encourage this game, I had to set the example. While referring to Romans 14:13, if we are causing offence and are approached by our brethren then we should honor their request and stop doing the offensive thing. It is after all, only righteous before the Lord.

I don't want to lead you into thinking that I was always the perfect youth leader. I am far from being perfect at anything. Something I've struggled with as a Christian is faithful attendance. I had heard from my youth "every time the doors of the church are open, you better be there." I know this is true, and I admit I have allowed other things besides work stand before my own attendance. Oh, I'm there every Sunday morning, no matter what, but other services I sometimes falter. I'd have my youth class at six thirty on Sunday night, and afterwards the worship service took place upstairs. In addition to having the class, I had also agreed to hauling kids back and forth to class. In order to get them and myself home early, I began leaving as soon as our lesson and playtime was over. You think this sounds innocent enough, well it's not. I would send a handful of the kids upstairs to their parents to stay through the sermon, while I and the rest of the crew would leave early. Does that sound like a good role model to you? Not really. One night the pastor called me on it. He lovingly stated that my leaving early right after class, was not setting a good example for our youth.

You know what, he was right, and I knew it. I spoke with the kid's parents I had been transporting and from that next Sunday on we stayed for preaching. It is absolutely the right thing to do for fellow Christians to point out mistakes being made by other believers. It is our job as Christians to acknowledge those mistakes, and willfully correct them. Constructive criticism as the world designates it. We shouldn't get angry or impudent, we should want to act accordingly to God's word so as not to offend our brothers and sisters. I never want to be a "stumbling block" toward anyone especially our youth. The apostle Paul even stated to the church at Corinth in 1 Corinthians chapter 1 verse 10: "Now I beseech you, brethren by the name of our Lord Jesus Christ, that ye all speak the same thing, and that there be no divisions among you; but that ye be perfectly joined together in the same mind and in the same judgement." I so have always admired the apostle Paul. He not only started all those churches, but frequently wrote to them, checked on them, and gave them feedback. He was never afraid to speak plainly if they were the slightest bit off track. We should do this for one another, in a loving manner as Christ rebuked his disciples. Remember folks God can and will use us to help others if we allow Him.

As the years passed, I decided to give up my youth ministry to a younger more able-bodied believer. He was eager to share his knowledge base from his years at Liberty University. My faithful sidekick, who has been a wonderful youth minister himself, joined forces and he and this young man have become quite the team. I'm proud of our youth and some have grown to accomplish wonderful things. I'm happy to report most are still attending church, both here and other areas where they live. I would encourage fellow believers to support them and have a passion for them as I still do. They are our hope and our future for sharing the gospel of Christ in this turbulent world.

CHAPTER 14

THE CARIBBEAN AWAITS

Seeing the title of this chapter you're probably thinking, "what in the world does this Ellie Mae from the hills, have to do with the Caribbean?" No, it wasn't a vacation, a typical beach trip for us mountain folk usually means hitting the Carolina coast. Did y'all know Myrtle Beach is considered the "Redneck Riviera?" Rightfully so, I love me some Carolina sunshine. I'm getting to my connection, trust me.

Another opportunity soon arose where God had planned to use me in a way I had never imagined. A close friend of mine at the time, a fellow nurse and a believer, approached me about wanting some time off. When she explained why, an immediate shock went through my system. Her Methodist church was sponsoring surgical nurses to fly down to Haiti, and care for those who had been injured in the earthquake. It was 2010 and Haiti had just undergone one of the worst earthquakes in human history. Hundreds of people were killed and thousands more wounded. There was a definite need for humanitarian aid on that tiny island so far from West Virginia. I could immediately feel God tugging at my heartstrings. I began asking her questions and after finding out more about the mission, she asked "would you like to go too?" "What? I couldn't leave my family, my job responsibilities, especially if we were going to be one nurse shy as it was. "Or could I?" I politely told her initially I would pray about it and speak to my husband. I needed to see if it would even be a remote possibility. A few weeks went by and I knew God was leading me on this trip. I had to go. No, my husband wasn't happy at first and naturally he feared for my safety. He had been military and had been out of the country before, "other countries aren't like ours," he said. God Bless America, I love my country and have learned from this experience and others to love it even more. Strife and turmoil may sometimes prevail, but this is still the greatest country on the planet.

So, the time was closing in for the departure date and my mind was made up. I was going to the mission field. Both excited and a little nervous, I began preparation. First up, I needed a passport. I went to the courthouse in our little town of Lewisburg, WV and retrieved all the necessary forms and attachments. I then took myself to the CVS pharmacy and had a passport picture taken. That's the great thing about small Appalachian towns, many businesses can do multiple things you wouldn't even expect. I soon had all the paraphernalia required, including a letter to one of our state governing officials in order to expedite the process.

I can remember getting out of the truck that day as a strong September east wind was blowing. Suddenly, before I could take any action, all my articles blew from my hands. As I'm scrambling down one of the little side streets above the courthouse in a panic and trying to collect everything, I began thinking. "How could you be thinking anything at a time like that," you ask? I distinctly recollect I was thinking "this is Satan, he is trying to deter me from making the trip, from listening to God's call." In response, I began quoting what my Savior said to Satan as he was tempting Jesus in the wilderness. In Luke 4:8, Jesus proclaimed "Get thee behind me, Satan: for it is written, "Thou shalt worship the Lord thy

God, and him only shalt thou serve". Thankfully by God's grace I was able to recover the forms I needed to complete the task. In just two weeks I received my passport and began to pack. We not only packed personal items, but also suitcases full of clothing and medical supplies our facility and physician's offices had donated. For example, things like gauze bandages, topical medications, IV cathlons, urinary catheters, IV tubing, and the list goes on. We were ready.

My nurse partner and friend picked me up early one morning as we made the first leg of our trek down to Charlotte, NC. All went well for our flight to Miami, then onto Port-au-Prince. What made it even sweeter is that the church sponsoring my friend donated two hundred dollars to help cover my cost of the airline ticket. I was not a member of their Methodist church, however, which proves a valid point. As fellow Christians join-together in order to help others, the task at hand should be non-denominational. In other words, God does not discriminate according to our religious sects, so why should we?

The flight to Miami and then to Port-au-Prince was uneventful, quite enjoyable really. The plane was one of the largest Boeing manufactures and was filled to the brim with passengers. I soon discovered most were medical professionals like me, as well as missionaries from a beloved organization called Samaritan's Purse. It felt amazing to be among this group whose sole purpose was to help this poor country deal with the aftermath of such a tragic circumstance. Once we landed, I must admit there had been nothing in my life up to this point to prepare me for what happened next. As we exited the plane and entered the crowded luggage area, you knew right away what it meant to be considered a third world country. It was a little frightful at first because of the chaos and shouting. Strange people, unfamiliar languages, dust blowing in from the streets, it almost felt as if I had been cast in an Indiana Jones movie. Determined to make the best of it and accomplish what God had willed me to do, I followed my friend as we stepped outside. It was hot, and that's an understatement. The humidity in Haiti was overwhelming compared to the climate in the West Virginia hills. I immediately began to sweat in every possible part of my anatomy. "Uuuugh, I should have brought more baby powder," I thought. There were also children shouting through a chain link fence as we made our way to the transport vehicle of a nearby guest center. They were loudly yelling "Seester, Seester," and reaching through the fence for a handout. My friend stated that their proclamation "Seester," was the only English they knew when it came to white American women. Immediately my heart broke for them, where were their parents? They had nothing, only themselves and one another.

Another shock to my system was operating a motorized vehicle in Haiti, meant no traffic laws. You basically just blow your horn and go. Jetting around in our guide's older model Suzuki Samurai, was an adventure in and of itself. No traffic lights, or road signs, just dirty dusty streets filled with pedestrians and other vehicles with lots of noticeable dents and bangs. Yikes!

Arriving at the guest house, I was soon told by other nurses and fellow healthcare workers to "lose the socks." You probably are wondering where on earth this statement came from, but let me just say, they were right. During the day you walked everywhere, that was your only means of transportation. The dusty litter filled streets were exactly what the Crocs manufacturers dreamed of when they created their product. Our first day began with some words of warning, as well as a tour of the guest house, the hospital, and the maternity center. It was stressed to us immediately not to go out into the streets at night. There were walls around each of the dwellings I mentioned, very impressive ones I might add. There were iron gates, and iron bars even above the walls. Then there were the dogs, the Mastiffs. Our missionary guides were fans of the breed due to their devoted guardianship. Already a dog lover, I was fascinated, not only by their size, but by their act of protection and fierceness when one of the uninvited Haitians would bang on the gates. And yet they were so gentle and loving when it came to the people they served. I have to say I immediately fell in love with the breed. Back to the subject at hand, we were only to travel during the day on foot from the guest house to the hospital, and only with accompaniment from one of the male attendants. Going out alone and without permission could be disastrous. No problem, I thought, I will most definitely be intent on obeying those rules.

I was first assigned as an orientee on the night shift. Twelve hours in a make-shift hospital, surrounded by rock walls and iron bars. The hospital beds were cots, some indoors, on the porches, and some outside in tents. We would hang IVs, do dressing changes, and comfort crying children by the headlamps that we wore. I soon became quite attached to the patients. Most of them had been there for quite some time, healing from their surgeries and wounds. There was a variety of Haitian folks there, both young and old. Some of the patients were suffering from catastrophic wounds and others were barely scathed. There were also those who had healed from their wounds, but unfortunately had no home to return to. The homeless were encouraged to stay at the hospital and help, at least until they could get back on their feet. It was, suffice it to say, a happy little community. One would never imagine that people so poor and had lost what little they had to be so content.

Let me tell you folks, nonverbal communication is important, especially when you don't know the language. Oh, I picked up a few words here and there, but not many. Haitians speak creole' which is a modified version of the French language. The French occupied nation had always been oppressed by their neighbors, very similar to modern day Israel. There were United Nations armed guards everywhere you went, and for some odd reason their appearance seemed ominous and not comforting. Unfortunately, most peace keeping authorities in Haiti were known to be corrupt as well as the government. It was obvious that the political leaders there cared nothing for the people and kept any monetary gain for themselves. Nevertheless, the overcrowding, the sickness, the destruction from the earthquake, had not dampened the spirit of a resilient people.

I became particularly close to many of the patients and workers. For example, one of the Haitian ladies assisting in the kitchen area had the most adorable toddler. In addition to our nursing duties, we were all makeshift nannies running around the compound keeping up with her cute self. Then there was our night interpreter whose French name I thought did not suit him, so I began to call him John after the disciple whom Jesus loved. He was always up for discussing Christ and the Bible stories we both held dear. Our patients were thriving and enjoyed our presence. We had a young mother, beautiful and sweet. She had a newborn daughter and had received injuries related to the birth. We cared for her daily, knowing sadly that she had HIV. The virus was very common in Haiti, and we all knew that the lasting effects and prognosis for those affected would not be desirable at best. Then there was my buddy, Raymone' which I dubbed Raymond, after a favorite American TV show character. He was a ten-year old prodigy who could easily brighten the world of those around him. We played cards and he would win, laugh at me and say "blanca", which means white in their language. We enjoyed our time together and he reminded me of my youth members back home.

All these relationships enriched my life, made me a better person, and helped me to recognize the blessings in even the small things. I remember sitting on the steps of the large porch and listening to the Haitian versions of some old English hymns. I would sing along in my own language and the tears would roll down my face. This emotional time was not homesickness, this was more of a feeling that I belonged. Even in a world far different from my own, God allowed me to fellowship with other believers. Spiritual unity, there's nothing like it.

Ultimately, the last day of our weeklong assignment had come. We were both feeling anxious to return home to our loved ones, but also saddened to leave the new friends we had made. It was agreed that we would take a quick tour of the city prior to heading to the airport. As we strolled the streets and remained close to our Haitian tour guides, the sights and sounds of the city inspired us. Among the crowds of poor Haitian families roaming to and from, many had no real place to call home. I remember thinking to myself, in God's eyes these people are important, and they are loved. I began praising God for the experience, when suddenly a tall Haitian fellow tapped me on the shoulder. I was startled at first, he was very tall, dark and had the whitest teeth I had ever seen. He began to question me in broken English "you be coming back to Haiti?" I smiled as I responded, "I hope too one day." He himself smiled and spoke in affirmation, "you be coming back to Haiti." As I turned to make certain I was still with the group, I quickly looked back within a few seconds and realized the large man had completely disappeared. He was just here, I thought. I asked my friend, "Hey did you see that man who was just here talking to me?" She gave me a look like "are you crazy," and shook her head no. From that day forward I knew God had sent an angel to encourage me, to enlighten me, and let me know that one day I would return to that special place. I haven't yet, but I will, "I will be coming back to Haiti."

"Be not forgetful to entertain strangers: for thereby some have entertained angels unawares". (Hebrews 13:2).

Six months had passed since my mission trip experience when a friend called me one day unexpectedly. She stated, “Roberta, there are mastiff puppies who need rescued.” “They are at the Humane Society and have been confiscated from a puppy mill.” “Would you like one?” God’s reward for a job well done. Our beautiful brindle girl Roxie is now nine years old and has been the sweetest blessing to us both.

“So that a man shall say, Verily there is a reward for the righteous: verily he is a God that judgeth in the earth.” (Psalms 58:11)

CHAPTER 15

ROUND TWO

Seven years had passed since my initial episode. God was continuing to bless me with opportunities to serve Him. Then early one Spring, I experienced a "blip." By blip I mean an unexpected noise on the radar, a deviation from a general trend. I can't remember if it was my counselor or my psychiatrist who once told me your first bout of depression is usually your worst. That part I believe is true. Unfortunately, I didn't take that information to heart. What do I mean you ask? It means after seven years of reveling in God's blessings and living the life I felt lead to live, I thought I was cured. So, I decided that I no longer needed the medication I was currently taking. I also took it upon myself to only commit to one last follow-up with my clinical psychiatrist. Why did I do this you wonder? I'd like to say stupidity, but probably shouldn't. Again, I was worried about the stigma attached. I had heard for years from other healthcare providers about the addiction, about the weakened state of the individual, and I didn't want to be identified with either of those categories. Gradually, I weaned myself off the antidepressant and had already allowed my prescription for the antianxiety medication to expire. Yeah, I was doing great, or so I thought.

I've heard that healthcare workers are weighed down by the

events they experience in their workplace. I must admit even though I love my job, there are times when sitting by the bedside of a patient who just learned they have advanced stage cancer can be heartbreaking and stressful. There are other gut-wrenching scenarios that I won't delve into, but you get my drift. It was early Spring when I began feeling a little pressured by life in general. Not to worry though because I knew warmer weather was coming, and I could once again be outdoors where I prefer to be. It was a sunny April Sunday after church, when my cousin, our mutual friend, and I decided to take an afternoon trail ride. It was warm, the trees were starting to bud, and life was good. I had taken along my young yearling colt that my cousin and I had rescued in the Spring of the previous year. "Show him the ropes," so to speak. So, she and I took turns ponying him alongside our adult horses, just so he could get the "trail experience." In our little small farming community where I grew up, everyone knows everyone. Happened to run into my cousin's uncle from the other side of family. Construction worker, farmer, man of the church, this fella wears a lot of hats. He told us he was moving cattle to Summer pastures. Usually, in our neck of the woods, cows get moved on foot with sticks, and sometimes with ATVs. We, however, were excited to get that "wild west" feel, so we asked if we could tag along on horseback. He said, "Sure." I thought it would be a great opportunity for my young horse who was bred to work cattle in the first place.

So, off we went on an adventure, several on foot, and the three of us on horseback. I decided here is where I can forget all my work woes and enjoy the things I really loved. I was more than happy spending the afternoon with friends, family, and getting a little saddle time in as well. Halfway up the mountain, I was encouraged to let my young horse wander along beside us without the lead rope. It seems as if he had a knack for moving cattle and would nip them, if they got to close. I was proud, he had lived up to his breeding. Things were going great, or so we thought.

The farmer's grandson had decided to tag along. He was coming nine years old and grew tired halfway up the mountain. It was a very long walk, through the woods, and then along the hardtop of the windy, curvy, one lane mountain road. So, my friends and I took turns hopping down from our horses in order to give the little fella a break and let him ride. We ambled along behind about thirty head of bawling cattle before we reached the top of the mountain, where the pasture was located. I was leading the young man on my best mare "Q" at the time. We stood back from the group which consisted of my cousin's uncle, the young man's parents, my cousin, my friend, and a few others. We waited and watched as the landowner opened the gates allowing the cattle to free roam the hillside.

Little did I know looming on the other side of my big mare, was my colt. He had been frolicking in the field below the gates where we stood. I had been watching the cattle enjoying their first taste of fresh Spring grass, when I caught movement from the corner of my eye. My young horse was wearing an old beat up saddle, once again to use for training purposes, and he somehow managed to tangle himself in the reins of my mare. The reins fell neatly over the horn of the saddle, and immediately began to pull tight. Foolishly I reached for the reins, when I should have reached for the boy. In an instant the young horse spooked and ran full speed down the middle of the one lane road. Praise God there is very little traffic on that mountain. I was still holding the lead rope, so I began running alongside my mare who had no choice but to follow the colt. At that point I was thinking if I can just get up to the saddle and reach the young man, I can pull him safely into my arms. The reins still firmly wrapped around the saddle horn; there we went flying down the mountain. Knowing

I couldn't keep up with horses for long, I pulled back hard on the lead rope, but to no avail. Being the wonderful rock-solid mare that she is, she couldn't stop, she wouldn't stop and risk the life of the young human screaming on her back. At that moment I tripped, fell, and was dragged approximately thirty feet on the pavement. I remember looking up as my horses sped off with someone else's child galloping full speed ahead. I started praying, Lord please protect them, please protect them. Thankfully, my friends had heard our cries and came riding hard in the runaway's direction. Before they could reach the blind curve ahead my friend said the young horse just stopped mid gallop, turned back to the field, and started grazing. Physically, I had only minor injuries. It wasn't the first time I had left a bit of my hide on a backroad. Emotionally, however, I was an absolute train wreck. I quickly ran to embrace he and my cousin who had just pulled him from the horse. We were all in tears. I apologized multiple times, only to be consoled by the parents and grandparent that these things do happen. Then the young man's father looked at me and said, "Roberta, I do believe there was an angel in that road, God sent him to stop the horses and save my son." I knew at that moment he was right. After all, we were all praying as it was happening. Praise God, He answers in the blink of an eye.

I walked the entire way down the mountain to my cousin's house, leading the horses and bawling like there was no tomorrow. Happy no one was hurt, praising God, but again feeling the guilt for what could have been a catastrophe. No one blamed me, it was a sudden and completely random event that struck terror in all involved. I couldn't help but think, however, what if the angel hadn't stopped those horses. Where would that boy be? Would he even be alive? And that my friends became my trigger for round two.

CHAPTER 16

PANIC

After several weeks and even months after the traumatic event, I was certain I had put it behind me. I was struggling to enjoy the events of an early Summer, and was starting to feel a creeping anxiety setting in. You know that "gnawing feeling in your gut" that I mentioned in an earlier chapter. Unfortunately, sometime after that wild ride that we took, my mare came down with a mysterious illness. She had limited mobility, profuse swelling in all four legs, and weakness in her hips. Over the period of about a week, her condition deteriorated. I rushed her to the vet on a Tuesday, after noticing the illness a few days before. That day she was so sick she could hardly leave the barn. I have a wonderful team of country vets who work relentless hours, and yet seem to find time to give each animal extraordinary attention. Unfortunately, my vet was baffled. I thought if anyone knows what may be going on it's her. She is a top shelf equine vet and has been an invaluable resource to me for many years. We discussed the event that happened that day on the ride and she decided no muscle or bone injuries could be involved. The injury would more than likely be isolated to only one limb or one area of the body. This was a more systemic illness. I explained to her that my farrier had commented on how she was having difficulty standing for him while he shod her, or for you non-horsey friends "applied shoes." She speculated a possible tickborne sickness and consulted Virginia Tech. All the initial testing came back negative, but all too often when caught early, bloodwork for tickborne illness is somewhat unreliable. She decided to treat for Lyme's disease or Anaplasma ultimately and I was to keep her under close observation. The early treatment seemed to be helping right away, but unfortunately it was doing a number on her liver. We had to switch antibiotics. The new means of treatment we hoped would be curative, but unfortunately took much longer to be effective.

It was during that time I spent the entire Summer just trying to get my best horse back. Giving injections, administering oral meds, and providing extra feedings for all the weight loss, consumed my evenings after work. It was a long road, but thankfully God let me keep my prize baby. Word to the wise, do all you can for your pets as far as tick prevention. It will save you from not only the expense, but from the sight of your beloved pet suffering. Also spay and neuter; I threw that one in for free.

Four months had gone by since I had stopped taking the antidepressants. I had a good run, but I could feel myself slipping back into an anxiety ridden state. One Friday evening I came home from work and my husband took one look at me and said, "It's happening again." This time I knew better than to argue, and I had already left a message at my psychiatrist office for an appointment as soon as possible. It was our date night, time for a meal and a movie. My husband thought it would be a good idea to keep my mind off things. Well it didn't help, not at all. I couldn't finish my Bob Evans country style beef stew, although I tried so my husband wouldn't see how far I had progressed. Thankfully during the meal, the psychiatrist office called back and had worked me into Monday's schedule. I had a long sigh of relief, but thought how in the world can I make it through the weekend? I began to feel my heart pound and I was sweating profusely, two ominous signs that my anxiety was beginning to affect my physical state. I didn't want to disappoint my husband, so I willingly went ahead to the movie. Mistake. The movie was an intense one, about war, romance, and tragedy. In my normal state of mind, I possibly would have thought it was a great production, but unfortunately it only made my condition even worse.

Up to this point I had never experienced a panic attack. I had heard patients speak of them and wondered how valid their stories really were. They seemed so dramatic. Let me tell you something panic attacks are for real. By the time I arrived home for the evening I was visibly shaking. I took a hot bath and tried some other coping methods, but to no avail. My heart was still racing to the point that I thought I may have to go to the emergency room for a ventricular episode. Then I let an old familiar fear creep in. "I know this is the anxiety talking. If I go to the ER now, what will my coworkers think, will I be considered unfit as a nursing leader?" My husband held me close that night, he could feel my body shaking and my heart pounding. As he drifted off, I knew that night would be a sleepless one for me. Where would I turn? I had to get through this somehow. I picked up my Bible beside my bed and headed to the spare bedroom. I sat there praying for some time, rocking back and forth, and then I opened that glorious book to hear God speak. I immediately turned to a favorite verse; (2 Timothy 1:7) "For God hath not given us the spirit of fear; but of power, and of love, and of a sound mind". That night that verse I held so dear became my mantra. I repeated it over and over in my head before I eventually fell asleep. God's word brings us the comfort we need. I encourage you to please read, memorize, and recite, that way no one can ever take it from you.

Mondays are generally not popular with most of us, but that following Monday was an answer to my prayers. At my appointment

I promptly agreed to return to my medicinal regimen as well as trying some mental exercises involving what I am most grateful for in life. Unfortunately, there is no quick fix for these episodes, and I found myself feeling more and more anxious.

It was October and I knew I had planned a short trip to Texas to visit my brother and his family. I was looking forward to seeing them and watching my niece and nephew play sports. Both are extremely athletic and excel in a variety of types, with baseball and softball being our family favorites. Most folks would have been excited to visit, and I was, but I soon found myself being filled with dread. It wasn't because I didn't love my extended family, or that I wouldn't be happy to see them. You see for a depressed and anxiety ridden person, the thoughts of leaving a familiar environment can be overwhelming. It seems that while we're away we lose control of our "little bubble." We constantly worry about the "what-ifs" that could happen if we're gone. Hard to enjoy the good times, when you're always dwelling on the bad, or the seemingly bad. I did go however, and had a really good time, only to return feeling more depressed.

Anxiety as I've said before, if allowed will lead to periods of depression. I had hit bottom once again. This time though I was ready, and I knew what to do to heal my troubled mind. I returned to my doctor, for further med adjustments and a little soul searching. She asked, "did you enjoy those kids so much that it brought back old feelings?" "Are you still longing for children yourself?" As we sat and talked, I did admit to the fact that I sometimes wonder what my life would be like with children of my own. Feeling that sense of pride when they accomplished great things. Experiencing happy times, when they brought joy and excitement. I also weighed the alternative, the incessant worry over their bad habits. Would they choose to ignore the righteous path of God and disobey their Dad and myself? What about as I grew older, what would happen? Would I be all alone in a nursing home? Would there be no one there to pluck my chin hairs because I could no longer see? Okay, maybe too much overthinking, yet another pitfall of depression and anxiety. She and I then began to discuss options. I have my nieces, nephews, and my young cousin, they could all rid those unwanted hairs. "I needed to focus on being a good mentor, and role model for them, I said." "I need to keep teaching compassion, a love for God, and fellow man." "I will repeat the exercise of naming off nine things I am grateful for in a day." You would be surprised at the people and the things you can come up with on that list. Praise God, I found it extremely helpful and was back on my game by the holidays. God is good, all the time!

CHAPTER 17

REVELATIONS

So, the previous episode that I explained, revealed to me I had a weakness. My faith and my trust in God, was not where it needed to be. I had planned a return trip to Haiti last January with the Samaritan's Purse Organization. Unfortunately, at that time, my mother had some medical issues pop up and I didn't feel I could leave her. Remember your yearly mammograms ladies, very important and may save your life. Also, there was an uprising in that poor nation and many outside countrymen were being asked to leave. "Okay Lord, I hear you, now is not the time". Here's where the patience comes in. My mother was being referred to many different doctors and to many different testing facilities. The news of the results took weeks and even months to arrive. As of late being on the other end of the healthcare spectrum through the eyes of a patient or a family member, you realize how much you need to be your own advocate. Sure, I had the knowledge of what it would take to get my mother where she needed to be, but the task at hand seemed overwhelming at times. I soon learned a new perspective, that as a healthcare worker I decided to apply in my own practice. It's simply a spin off on the golden rule, "Treat all patients as if they are your own parent, precious family member, or yourself." This was my take on the whole process. After all the numerous phone calls, requests for test results, addressing some oversights, I realized we need to be an advocate for all our patients and not forget what being a nurse is truly about. Finally, her surgery took place, everything went well, and the recovery was remarkable. Of course, frequent follow ups are necessary. She is still undergoing treatment for the illness, but God is right there. Each time the fear is malignancy, but up to this point each pathology report has returned benign. God's grace in action, prayer at work, and patience in all things.

"Be still, and know that I am God: I will be exalted among the heathen, I will be exalted in the earth". (Psalms 46:10)

Going forward to the present I realize my life is not my own, it's God's. He has blessed me tremendously with more friends than I could imagine, a job I love, and the little hobby farm that I call home. When you follow His instruction and be intent on becoming the person God wants you to be, then life has much more meaning. I go to work daily helping others, only to find I'm the one being blessed. I frequently trail ride with some very close friends on the weekends where we talk things out and and discuss daily issues. Having true friends that will stick by you through thick and thin, is a gift in and of itself. My husband and I now share a better, stronger relationship. He now seems to understand what I was going through with the depression, and I feel that I no longer need to hide those feelings when they present themselves. My life or anyone else's for that matter will never be perfect, because we are not perfect. God will still allow the devil to send fiery trials that mold us and make us who He desires us to be. The key is to accept that God is with you no matter what. Stand against those temptations that Satan may send to sway you. Believe me he can take something that seems so innocent and use it against you.

It was in between my two major episodes when I was tempted twice by Satan. I suppose his thinking was this, if "I can't get to her through the anxiety and depression, I will try another means to destroy her testimony."

My husband and I are alike in some ways, but then again very different in others. Our longstanding relationship had reached a point where we were arguing a good bit mainly over finances, the usual things couples fight about. I had been blessed by God to be able to purchase my grandad's property from my uncle, and I had an innate desire to build and move there. My husband however, desired to remain on his family's land where we currently reside. The disagreements went on for several weeks, even months, and would get very heated at times. My reasoning to move was that I feel more comfortable and more at home in a place less populated. I would have more trails to ride and grazing for my horses. In that, I failed to remember that ever important verse; "Let your conversation be without covetousness; and be content with such things as ye have: for he hath said, I will never leave thee, nor forsake thee."

For now, we have a system in place, and will continue to reside here where it is more convenient to commute to work. I utilize my portion of grandad's place to farm and produce hay, which saves on cost. There is still time to think about relocating in the future. After all, marriage is about compromise and arguing rarely accomplishes anything productive.

"Wherefore they are no more twain, but one flesh. What therefore God hath joined together, let not man put asunder." (Matthew 19:6)

There was also another time, that I had experienced Satan's sabotage. He's a destroyer and a cunning enemy, be very watchful in the things that you do and say. My husband and I had shared a mutual friendship with a man who my husband had worked with for many years. When this gentleman was married, we would often visit each other as couples. After a period of many years, this fella who I must say is "as good as gold," had lived through two disappointing relationships. One day my husband came home from working at his new job telling me that he had ran into his former coworker and friend. He stated, "that he felt bad for him," and "that he was now going through a second divorce." Together we decided we would invite our friend over for dinner and attempt to cheer him up. After all that's what friends do. Throughout the evening it was obvious that our friend was feeling extremely low. So low in fact that I began to be concerned for his welfare. A few days had passed and although I had been praying earnestly, I felt led to shoot him a text. I wanted to check on him and get a feel for his state of mind after our last encounter. Do you remember me saying that once you go through depression God allows you to be keenly aware of others who may be going through similar or even more intense circumstances? The reply he sent revealed the truth, he was struggling and finding it harder each day to make it through. I shared with him about the God we love, and he attested to being saved, but felt he needed to have a closer relationship with the Savior. So, we continued texting over the next several days. I began sharing with him some encouraging words and scriptures. Soon the days soon turned into weeks, months, until finally a year had passed. We had become close friends by this time and things seemed innocent enough. I must admit, however, I had felt the sting of the Holy Spirit convicting me much earlier and I didn't take heed.

I knew in my heart what the Bible stated about not necessarily texting mind you, but even being seen or heard speaking to another man or woman in a close relationship. Even though in no way was there any physical involvement, I had allowed myself to become close to a man other than my husband. Satan had used my gift of compassion for others against me. How you might ask? By caring deeply for another individual, which in and of itself is not wrong, but because it was another male, I felt as if some form of adultery had occurred. In Matthew 5:28 the Bible states, that whosoever looks upon another hath committed adultery already in their hearts. Looking, texting, not a lot of difference there. I quickly confessed to God, my husband, and to the man I was intent to help. He agreed, and we are still good friends, but no further communication occurs other than exchanging pleasantries. I'll never regret reaching out to him in his time of need. I believe God wants us to share His message of hope no matter what. Fellow believers just be wary of certain situations. As I've stated earlier, "sin can take you farther than you want to go."

We have indeed come to the final chapter of my personal story. It is here I'll reveal the things I have learned from the guilt, the depression, and the anxiety ridden experiences. Ultimately my goal here is to help someone struggling with similar or possibly even the worst of circumstances. I've comprised a list of the things that have helped me understand and have given me the ability to cope.

1. Go immediately to God without question
2. Never give up and persevere
3. Be open minded in determining causative factors
4. Never let the opinions of others cloud what you know is best
5. Seek professional help, use counseling and if necessary, medication
6. Use the experience as a tool to grow your faith
7. Share your testimony with others who may be seeking help
8. Never be afraid to approach someone and ask if they are depressed, (You may just save a life)
9. Be mindful always of your behavior and know your triggers
10. Help others by sharing the gospel of Christ

11. Don't allow Satan to use your strengths or your weaknesses against you
12. Stand strong in your beliefs, but do not allow yourself to pass judgement

I have chosen to share my innermost thoughts and feelings with those of you who are wandering in the darkness. Some of these moments I must admit I'm not actually too proud of. These are however, the raw "nitty gritty" everyday moments of a believer struggling to cope with the guilt and shame of depression. I'm here to say life goes on and there is most assuredly a light at the end of the tunnel. So, keep searching, be patient, and wait on God. He is likely allowing this trial of depression to submerge you in order to show you how to live a better way. His way. Please don't allow the guilt that you yourself may feel or the judgement of others weigh you down further. It makes for a much harder and much longer recovery. Never allow someone to belittle your feelings. However silly they may seem they are real to you. Until someone is in the depths of the despair, they may never know what you are experiencing. Severe depression as I've mentioned, can cloud your judgement, but remember to continue to value yourself. "I will praise thee; for I am fearfully and wonderfully made: marvelous are the works; and that my soul knoweth right well."(Psalms 139:14) Remind yourself that although it may be difficult in the darkness, you will once again blossom in God's service. Most importantly, be mindful that even though others around you may fail you, God never will.

CHAPTER 18

DEAR DOUBTERS

"Haters gonna hate", isn't that what all the cool kids are saying? I wouldn't know I was never a "cool kid," and now in my late forties I'm certainly not a kid period. What I'm saying in this chapter is this. There will always be people who doubt you, your mental health illness, your treatment plan, and the list goes on. The Bible tells us "Let nothing be done through strife or vainglory; but in lowliness of mind let each esteem other better than themselves." (Phil 2:3) Yes, we've all been guilty of passing judgement on fellow believers and unbelievers alike. Those times when you have found yourself thinking, "what is wrong with him or her," "is he or she crazy?" The essence of the friction between those who have experienced depression and those who have not, is lack of knowledge. You've heard the expression "knowledge is power" or how about "experience is the best teacher." Those come in to play very well in this situation and I firmly believe that understanding is the key.

As I've discussed in earlier chapters there is a multitude of reasons mental illness exists. Genetics, traumatic experiences (both mental and physical), and certain other diagnoses can all be interchanged with signs and symptoms that can be confusing for even experts in the field of psychology. As Christians we sometimes become narrow minded in our views and opinions of others. How one should act or represent themselves as a believer is undeniably important, equally important is how we treat others in distress. Speaking to those who are Christians and are dealing with a friend or family member experiencing depression you must ask yourselves, "Is this the person I know and love?" "What changes are taking place here?" "Why are they completely off their game?" It's generally not hard to spot when someone you know so well is showing signs of depression. I mentioned a portion of the symptoms in an earlier chapter. They are changes in eating and sleeping habits, lack of interest, tearfulness, and listlessness. Irritability, fatigue, forgetfulness, and lack of focus are a few more ailments that can inhibit a person's normal routine. The most important thing for a friend or family member to take note of is, "what am I going to do about it?"

I'm sure it's extremely difficult being on the other side of things. As a matter of fact, I know, because I've been there too. The person or persons closest to the depressed individual are attempting to process exactly what is going on. For example, is this just a period of "feeling down" that will pass quickly or is this a more serious case of clinical depression. Failure to act as a support person can make or break a depressive episode for your loved one. Most spouses, parents, friends, are afraid of offending the individual during the initial approach. They're worried that their family member or friend may have an angry outburst, deny the situation, stop speaking to them or experience some other undesirable treatment. Perhaps as I spoke of earlier, they lack education. They may not recognize the signs, know where to seek help, or how to navigate the vast amount of information presented in a myriad of ways. My husband, bless his heart, would say things like "I've been having really crazy dreams and they're all about losing you." "I reach out in an effort to grab you, and you just disappear into thin air." He in other words, knew something was terribly wrong, but didn't know how to go about fixing it. Undoubtedly, God was sending messages to those around me. Fortunately, I had the blessing of having my mother who had experienced it herself and saw how it affected others in the family. She "got the ball rolling," so to speak in getting me the help I needed. My poor husband was eager to assist and soon got a "crash course" on navigating the illness of depression and how it changed from day to day.

The third reason could simply be that the support person is experiencing the same feeling of shame or disappointment. "How will it look to the family?" "How will it reflect on me being their loved one?" "If I report or bring to light the illness my loved one is experiencing will it damage their reputation or mine?" Each of these reasons are valid but sound somewhat selfish, don't they? Make certain your thought processes only benefit the person experiencing the illness and not how it will affect you, your home, your family, your church, or any aspect of your wellbeing. Don't make this about you. Unfortunately, I've seen some seemingly narcissistic reasoning for failing to come to someone's aide. An example is, "she's not paying the bills like she's always done, so I'm not responsible for the debt that we're in." Another could be, "he lost his job because he couldn't maintain his focus, how will I be able to keep up with my gym membership?" Sounds a bit harsh or ridiculous, but I want people to realize that marriage or any other type of relationship means supporting one another no matter what they're going through. I'm here to tell you, never let your pride interfere in caring for another's welfare. The Bible verse "And whosoever shall exalt himself shall be abased; and he that shall humble himself shall be exalted," (Matthew 23:12) serves as a reminder. It's not about you, it's about someone you love. Don't be afraid to intervene in any way, especially if you know they can be a danger to themselves. Caregivers I'm speaking directly to you, even if the person you love is in denial and refuses initially, do not give up. Continue to pray and address it with people who have the clinical knowledge, and only then you will receive God's desired outcome.

"And be ye kind one to another, tender hearted, forgiving one another, even as God for Christ's sake hath forgiven you." (Ephesians 4:32)

"Let us therefore follow after the things which make for peace, and things wherewith one may edify another." (Romans 14:19)

"For this is the message that ye heard from the beginning, that we should love one another." (1 John 3:11).

"For, brethren, ye have been called unto liberty; only use not liberty for an occasion to the flesh, but by love serve one another." (Galatians 5:13)

I could go on quoting verse after verse on this topic and how important it is for anyone dealing with a loved one to act on their instincts and seek help. One verse struck a chord for me in (Ecclesiastes 4:10); "For if they fall, the one will lift up his fellow: but woe to him that is alone when he falleth; for he hath not another to help him up." This verse speaks volumes. We need to be there for others in all capacities of our roles as Christians. Whether we be family or friends, teachers, ministers, or simply acquaintances. Everyone is equally important to God. The Bible states that we as Christians should be "Christ like" in our daily walk. So, knowing this we should adopt the same outlook as Jesus, we should love and respect our brethren. "With all lowliness and meekness, with longsuffering, forbearing one another in love;" (Ephesians 4:2)

It's tough sometimes being a Christian man or woman sitting in the congregation and hearing a teacher, pastor, or evangelist call anxiety a sin. Even though the Bible states "Behold the fowls of the air for they sow not, neither do they reap, nor gather into barns;

yet your heavenly Father feedeth them. Are ye not much better than they?" This verse screams the fact that God is reassuring and redirecting our anxiety or worry over to Him, after all He has promised to provide for us. I'm not here to dispute that in some cases anxiety may be sin. For example, when Adam and Eve sinned in the garden, they were "worried for their nakedness," or in other words exposure of sin towards God. They clearly had sinned against God and the worry was a direct result of that. But what about those of us who have a disorder?

There is no doubt that experiencing the despair taught me how to be a better Christian. Perhaps even some of the pride and discontentment I felt was directly related to the initial meltdown. How about the consecutive ones? Was I sinning each, and every time? I shudder to think of it all as punishment from God. After all we have loving God who understands our human nature. I have a hard time believing He wasn't right there beside me every time, through the ups and downs, and the hills and valleys. I've already established God is holy and can't look upon sin. His presence during those episodes I experienced were very evident, leading me to believe that it truly was not always a result of sin. So, unless one has the innate ability to get inside another's head how can you justify sin as the probable cause for each event.

I must say, neither do I appreciate those who condemn counseling and medication therapy. There of some of us who must obtain assistance in order to get back to the person we once were or whom God wants us to be. Maybe there are even some of you as Christian leaders, who are feeling the depths of despair and for a split second consider getting help. You're slipping you know you have been, and you can feel it. God is speaking to you through the darkness. You're wondering about your effectiveness towards Him and towards the people you lead. You may find yourself pushing this thought aside and going back to the old excuse, "what will others think of me?" Trust me it's not about what others think, it's what God thinks that matters. There are even Christian counselors who have been led by God to help others in this capacity. May I personally offer a suggestion? Please by all means allow them to fulfill their pledge to God and get the help you so richly deserve.

I also recognize the concern of all in religious leadership oftentimes is taking the medication. Trust me I know very well we are facing a national crisis, the opioid epidemic. I've seen it many times in my workplace. You learn as a healthcare provider very quickly to differentiate between compliant patients and those who fall victim to this terrible addiction. Here in the mountain state, it has received national recognition, and is a "hotbed" topic to many political as well as religious leaders. Truly it is a concern, however, there is a separation here, "those who need it" and "those who want it."

Most of the anti-anxiety and antidepression drugs do not fall in the opioid categories. Generally, they are Benzodiazepines and the many different types of antidepressants. SSRIs, Tricyclics, MAOIs, and Norepinephrine Reuptake Inhibitors to name a few. Each one targets individual brain chemicals that are either producing too rapidly or are lacking in production. Granted some of these can be addictive as well, and we learn from the start of engaging in this therapy what to watch for. We are carefully educated by our physicians and pharmacists to adhere to the prescription and take the dosage only as recommended. As I've stated before when it comes to treating depression, what works for one person may not work for another. So, don't be surprised when you see multiple meds being used initially. Finding the right drug for someone's depression can take time. Be careful not to judge and say things like "Oh they just want to be comfortably numb," "They're taking way too much," or "they just don't want to deal with life in general." It can take at least six weeks for an antidepressant to work fully, so please be mindful of one another's feelings during this time.

It can be an extremely frustrating period in the life of a depressed person. As if the illness wasn't debilitating enough, condemning a possible cure can literally push someone to the brink of despair. If you as a religious leader have never felt the angst and depression personally, then you must trust in your fellow believers. We truly don't want to feel this way, it steals our joy, ruins our relationships, and renders us helpless at times. I'm typically not one to be easily offended, but others are, and their confidence can be shattered by those whom they admire. I say with assurance and without hesitation, preach the fire and brimstone because that's what gets folks saved. I'm not upholding sugarcoating the truth by any means. I'm merely saying be a supporter, not a condemner when it comes to illnesses affecting the mind. We are all saved by God's grace through his son Jesus Christ, and "not of works, lest any man should boast." (Ephesians 2:9)

Jesus himself certainly didn't turn away the woman at the well, the adulterous woman facing stoning, the man possessed by demons. He willfully allowed himself to approach these people knowing what the Pharisees might say or think. He did it not to condemn, but to help them in each circumstance. "For God sent not his Son into the world to condemn the world; but that the world through him might be saved". (John 3:17) We as the church, leaders and congregation alike, need to unite to help the suffering of individuals within the church and in the communities surrounding us. Please know that I love and respect each church leader that has ever been in my life, both past and present. I value their teachings and admonition for God. Not all leaders or believers feel as if problematic anxiety is sinful, but others seem to disagree. Personally, I do however, feel very strongly that God has laid this message on my heart. A message of hope and understanding, rather than judgement and condemnation. I'm speaking not only to educate others, but to preserve the unity and the love for one another within our local churches and beyond.

"Behold, how good and how pleasant it is for brethren to dwell together in unity!" (Psalms 133:1)

"Endeavouring to keep the unity of the Spirit in the bond of peace. (Ephesians 4:3)

"Till we all come in the unity of the faith, and of the knowledge of the Son of God, unto a perfect man, unto the measure of the stature of the fulness of Christ:" (Ephesians 4:13)

CHAPTER 19

SIMPLE TRUTHS

How many times must we face adversity? One never knows, it is a true mystery of God. We can, however, take those harrowing experiences as I've mentioned earlier and use them for God's glory. Sometimes it seems as if it can be a "domino effect." First one troubling thing happens, and then another, and another. Please remember God's promises through it all; "These things I have spoken unto you, that in me ye might have peace. In the world ye shall have tribulation: but be of good cheer; I have overcome the world." (John 16:33) I love that verse of scripture because it gives us total reassurance that no matter what happens God ultimately has control. He wins, not Satan in the end. We already know this, so why do we fret?

I believe the way of the world sets in, the rushing around, the constant badgering of timelines, bill paying, and little to no downtime. In addition to those we experience conflict among ourselves, family quarrels, co-workers failing to "pull their weight," criticism from leadership, and marital discord. So, how do we as Christians deal with all those things and not become depressed or anxious? If the bad outweighs the good, then we can fall short of our best intentions and succumb to the darkness. The Bible says we don't have to. In Micah 6:8, the prophet reveals to us the simple truth. "He hath shewed thee, O man, what is good; and what doth the Lord require of thee, but to do justly, and to love mercy, and to walk humbly with thy God." Could it be that simple? Can those requirements that the world weighs heavy on our backs, be resolved with only those three things that the Lord asks us for? I think so, let me explain.

If we are remaining in the will of God for our lives, the Holy Spirit will guide us. We will be concerned with always doing the "right thing," by knowing how to act in any given situation. "Doing justly" is always being mindful that we are not perfect, however, knowing we must strive to be as much like Christ in everything we do. I believe, as I've mentioned before, that this principle is the perfect will of God. Jesus "acted justly" in the case of Zacchaeus. Do you remember this beloved tale from our vacation Bible school lessons? The epitome of an "oldie but a goodie." That rich rascal had obtained his money by cheating the Jewish people during tax time. Talk about unjust. Maybe he had "short man syndrome" and felt he was entitled. Nevertheless, he had heard the Savior was to pass that day through Jericho and by conviction I'm certain, he climbed that Sycamore tree to seek out Jesus. Even though the crowd was hard pressed, Jesus singled out Zacchaeus because he knew that there was an innate desire for goodness in that man's heart. A favorite Bible story for the kiddos, teaches a hard lesson for us as adults, Jesus commanded "make haste, and come down; for today I must abide at thy house." (Luke 19:5) Jesus made a just man out of Zacchaeus that day, even though the Pharisees criticized Him for going to the house of a man with an ill reputation. That was not the first time he had dealings with "unjust folks", mind you, I love the fact that Jesus did not discriminate. Zacchaeus then in verse 8 declared restitution: "Behold Lord, the half of my goods I give to the poor; and if I have taken anything from any man by false accusation, I restore him fourfold." A statement that is proof positive that Zacchaeus was sincere in his commitment to Christ. Not only did Zacchaeus receive salvation that day, but his entire household was dedicated in their belief as well.

Restoration my friend, comes from striving to be just. As Christians we can rest easier knowing the things that we did that day involved following Christ's example. As I've stated before when dealing with depression, sleep is sometimes a precious commodity. Isn't it grand knowing that when you lay your head down at night that you can rest easy and feel the peace that only God can give? Is it a comfort to know that you did your absolute best with the Holy Spirit's guidance in determining "the right thing," and finding resolution in such troubling circumstances? I hope my friends for your sake that it is.

A personal example of this goes back a few years and yes ironically it involves taxes. My husband and I have an aversion to doing our own. Neither of us are "math oriented" people, and with different funding and investment plans our yearly task had become quite complicated. We had decided to have a commercial tax preparer do the dreaded deed, thinking they would know best how to navigate the myriad of forms that came in the mail. My only job was to collect them all, easy right? We had been going to the same preparer year after year, so we assumed there would be no surprises as to the outcome of our filing. That particular year we delivered all the necessary items and waited for our tax preparer to contact us upon completion. Unfortunately, the call came and was not quite the news I expected. Instead of, "your tax returns are ready," it was "by the way we think a mistake has been made on last year's tax returns and the money you received as a refund was not warranted." "What", I replied, "I'm going to jail you say?" My mind was reeling, how could I have cheated the government, that is the one fear I held as reason enough to have my taxes done for me. So much for that idea. Then out of nowhere the mind-blowing reply came, "No you're not going to jail, we will let this go, it's likely not going to be found if the IRS hasn't found it by now." Wow, and I thought my mind was reeling before. What a suggestion. You see they were hoping for a cover up. In other words, "we got you the money, so there's no need to report and ruin both our reputations." "Let's all just look the other way." I thought to myself, "that's not going to happen!" I marched myself into the office and demanded my W-2s. Yes, it would have been so easy just to keep the money, especially since everyone else was so on board with hiding it. However, I knew in my heart it was wrong and would be sinful. Not to mention that the IRS has years of backlogged tax returns, so it could take months before any errors may be found. Truth be told, I feared God's punishment much more than the IRS. I learned a great deal in that six months of managing "tax return failure," so much so that I now feel comfortable doing my own. It was rough paying back what it had cost us, but we slept much better knowing the Holy Spirit was keeping us on the "just path."

Mercy, that glorious word we all know and love. God's goodness towards us even though we deserve nothing good. The Bible says "Our righteousnesses are as filthy rags; and we all do fade as a leaf; and our iniquities, like the wind, have taken us away." (Isaiah 64:6) Yet God chose to provide hope and a home in heaven through his son Jesus Christ. That my friends, is the epitome of mercy. All the wrong that I have done, I confess to God and he forgives me, yet I struggle sometimes to forgive myself. As a matter of fact, the sin in my life even upon confession, could have so easily been attributed to the guilt I felt during my depression. My anxiety could have been a result of self-punishment, a refusal to accept forgiveness in my own self. Like Christ forgives us, we must forgive ourselves. Some folks, like myself, find that very thing extremely hard to do.

I had a friend, an elderly gentleman, stand up in church one Sunday morning to give his testimony. He talked about "selling some of his wares on the side of the road." You might find this silly, a roadside flea market. But let me tell you us mountain folk see it as a golden opportunity for a favorite pastime, to barter and trade. "One man's trash is another man's treasure," so to speak. Ask my husband, he hits every auction, yard sale, flea market he can find. I must say he has brought home many interesting items over the years. Some quite useful, and some I might say, well we'll just leave it at that. Anyway, back to the story. My friend had been sitting by his truck for some time waiting for his first customer to arrive. He stated he began praying and asking God to send someone that he could witness to. It wasn't long after the prayer that a young man stopped by and inquired about something he had brought to sell. They began talking, I'm sure about guns or trucks, what most men discuss in these parts. My friend then stated that he had gotten so caught up in the conversation that he forgot all about the prayer he had just prayed. As the young man drove off, he said "I just dropped my head, I knew I had failed God, and let Satan intervene." He stated that he had confessed the oversight over and over to God, but just couldn't shake it. How many of us has ever done that? I know I have missed countless opportunities to be a witness and felt miserable about it. Immediately after he finished, I stood up. God, I knew, had given me the words to speak. I referenced his newly given testimony, and stated, "we ask God to forgive us and He does, but then the one thing we fail to do is to forgive ourselves."

How did I come up with this bit of wisdom, you ask? Surely not of myself, but because of God's unfailing love and mercy. The love and mercy He had shown to me during my time in the dark corners of depression. I was speaking from experience to someone twenty-six years my senior. Seems odd doesn't it, like it should be the other way around. Listen to what I'm saying, use those depression and anxiety ridden episodes to enrich your life, along with the lives of others. Draw what you can from those experiences. As I've said before, during those times it's hard to see the justification of it all or the possibility that anything good could come from this. Looking back, however, the lessons become clearer. Use those encounters and learn to show mercy not only to others, but to yourself. Forgive as Jesus spoke in Matthew 18:22, "I say not unto thee, Until seven times: but, Until seventy times seven."

Interestingly, following that verse in Matthew 18, Jesus told his disciples a parable. In Sunday school we learn a parable is "an earthly story with a heavenly meaning." Parables teach us valuable lessons of things spiritual, in relation to something here on earth that we can easily understand. This unique parable described a certain king who had loaned his servants "talents," or I presume money. The one servant owed ten thousand talents, a great sum of money. Unfortunately, the servant did not have the money to pay back the loan, so the king ordered that he be sold along with his wife and children. Undoubtedly, the servant knew the stakes were high that he could be sold to someone heartless and cruel, or that he and his family could somehow be separated during the transition. Speculation there on my part. So, the servant began begging for forgiveness and fell at his feet even in order to show the king his sincere apologies. Verse twenty-seven states: "Then the lord of that servant was moved with compassion, and loosed him, and forgave him the debt". The story ends there right, a happy ending. Sadly, no it does not. Jesus goes on to say, that same servant who had received forgiveness and relinquished his debt, did something irreconcilable. Verse twenty-eight: "But the same servant went out and found one of his fellowservants, which owed him an hundred pence: and he laid hands on him, and took him by the throat saying, Pay me that thou owest". You see we need to be careful, because history often repeats itself. That very same servant failed to offer forgiveness unlike his master, and when his fellow servant asked for patience for the payback due, the king's servant cast him into prison. As you might have guessed, the old king found out about the situation and "delivered him to the tormentors, till he should pay all that was due unto him." My Granny's saying rings true, "what goes around, comes around." The world calls it Karma, let them think what they will, we Christians know the truth. "Dearly beloved, avenge not yourselves, but rather give place unto wrath: for it is written, Vengeance is mine; I will repay, saith the Lord." (Romans 12:19)

It is God's mercy for us that should trigger our mercy to another human being. It's hard to forgive the wrong that's been done to you, but please by all means, trust the verse I quoted above about vengeance, it is most assuredly true. You make it much harder to live through the pain, the guilt, the depression, when you constantly dwell on the anger you feel toward yourself or someone else. Bitterness sets in and it makes the angst and misery nearly impossible to overcome. In order to round out that chapter of Matthew 18, Jesus spoke this; "So likewise shall my heavenly Father do also unto you, if ye from your hearts forgive not every one his brother their trespasses." (Matthew 18:35) May His Love of Mercy endure forever and dwell within you and me.

Humility, one we all struggle with from time to time. What does it mean to be humble you might ask? To be meek and lowly, not thinking too highly of one's self. The Bible serves up a ton of scripture dealing with being a humble servant of God. Humility is very high on my list as one of the more desired traits of Christianity, but many times I fall short. King Solomon gives us a gentle reminder in the book of Proverbs 15:33; "The fear of the Lord is the instruction of wisdom; and before honour is humility." Also, in

Proverbs 22:4 he states: "By humility and the fear of the Lord are riches, and honour, and life". Being humble should most certainly be something we should strive for first and foremost as Christians. It's the lack of humility, however, and the pride we feel that many times undermines our abilities. We fail to see ourselves as we really are, imperfect sinners. We often hide those imperfections, so those around us can uphold us, and praise our accomplishments. Isn't that where we go wrong in dealing with our mental health issues? Are you holding back on getting the help you need just so you can "save face?" We've discussed this in previous chapters so I'm not going to be redundant here, but please ask yourself this question; "are you letting your dignity stand between yourself and your healing?" As a Christian, you've confessed to humble yourself before a mighty God, why not practice humility when it comes to your peers? Haven't we already established His ways are higher than ours, in Isaiah 55:9. Who are we as humans, really? We are His creation, not the other way around. You go to God in prayer with your depressive affliction. Why should we be afraid to show our true feelings amongst others? He is the one who matters. The opinions of others should not concern us when it comes to our mental wellbeing. How can we compare the love and compassion of a Perfect God to the disapproval of an imperfect world?

Humility, something we hold in high esteem, but find ever so difficult to attain. Another of Jesus' parables described it best. In the book of Luke chapter 18, we see the parable of the Pharisee and the publican. Jesus told this parable in order to address certain ones which trusted the fact they were "more righteous" and despised all others because of it. His story began simply as two men entering the temple to pray. The Pharisee spoke first and made a dramatic display of how he thanked God that he was "not an extortioner, unjust, adulterer, or even as the publican." "Hello," the publican, also known as a tax collector, was standing within earshot. "Really dude?" "That was bold." Meanwhile the publican himself could not even look up, but "smote his breast" meaning he was terribly upset and sorrowful. "God be merciful to me a sinner;" he said in verse thirteen. Jesus then gave us the lesson for this story by summing it up in verse fourteen. "I tell you, this man (publican) went down to his house justified rather than the other: for every one that exalteth himself shall be abased; and he that humbleth himself shall be exalted."

Jesus himself shows humility in the account of John chapter 13. He humbly served his disciples by washing their feet during the Last Supper. A seemingly humiliating task reserved for the lowest of servants, it was a chore undoubtedly necessary due to dwelling in a dry and dusty desert setting. That's what makes it dramatically persuasive when you see Jesus performing such an act. In John 13:13-14 Jesus states "Ye call me Master and Lord: and ye say well; for so I am. If then, your Lord and Master have washed your feet; ye also ought to wash one another's feet."

While overcoming the clutches of depression, Jesus has revealed to me that it is really that simple. I can combat Satan, survive each state of despondency, and live according to the perfect will of God. Placing aside my imperfections, offering forgiveness, and refusing to look down on others, is a constant struggle. It does, however, keep my mind busy reminding myself what is truly important in life. He has shown me by living or should I say, "striving to live," according to these three relatively simple truths that I can face all life's adversity.

1. Do Justly
2. Love Mercy
3. Walk Humbly with thy God

CHAPTER 20

J.O.Y.

(Jesus First, Yourself Last, and Others In-Between)

True Joy is a feeling of elation, total happiness. I must admit it's extremely hard being in the depths of depression to even imagine feeling those emotions again. You begin to miss the joy and even crave it, but it seems so out of reach. You know in your heart of hearts that God is the source of true joy and being in His will gives us peace. So, why can we not attain it? Please believe me when I say I am no expert. I'm simply here to share with you the experiences I've had success in overcoming the darkness of depression. I know everyone is different, designed that way by our almighty God. In knowing this, I also know what works for me, may or may not work for you the reader. Not only are we all different as human beings, but we've had different life experiences as well. For example, I suffer from a genetic tendency which means I'm prone to have chemical imbalances in the brain. I have no authority in telling someone else who has been through a traumatic experience or experiences how to feel or what to think. I feel completely inadequate addressing a young girl who may have been abused or neglected. Not to mention a soldier who has been in a life or death situation during combat. I only know that you go to Jesus first, and assuredly the rest will fall into place. I do, however, offer suggestions throughout this testimony of mine that have worked in bringing back the joy. I want to devote this chapter itself as a showcase for what has helped me the most during those dark times.

Putting it simply, it's the act of helping others. It matters not the capacity in which you help, we can simply just sit and listen to someone. Sometimes just laying all your burdens out there in front of someone can help a troubled mind seek a solution. Oddly enough, one can often find resolution when they hear themselves speak it out loud. The person that's listening doesn't always have to speak. Instead, allow yourself as the listener to become intent and immersed in what they're telling you and completely shut out all distractions. Of course, you offer to seek professional help for them and for some that is absolutely warranted. But there are those that for whatever reason, time constraints or lack of funding maybe, who simply are not able to obtain clinical therapy. That is where being a good listener comes in. Sorting through the "ugly stuff," you can help them formulate a plan or prioritize those things that really matter in their life. Knowing that someone cares enough to listen is sometimes all a person needs.

The title of this chapter Jesus first, Yourself Last, and Others in Between, again comes from my early years in Sunday school. I remember teachers writing this on chalkboards, explaining the root of Joy comes from this simple foundation. I now write it on a dry erase board for my class of middle schoolers, explaining this is the key for living a successful Christian life. I try to live by this rule, and it has certainly seen me through some hard times. Helping others and putting them ahead of myself has been an excellent therapy for me and still is. I do want to emphasize however, there is an exception to this rule. Yes, always put Jesus first, but sometimes you must put yourself before others and seek treatment. You need to be "the best you" before you can be of any valuable assistance to someone in need. Make certain your mental stability is strong enough to withstand the tension others can create. You don't always have to be "completely healed." Nine times out of ten none of us will ever be completely healed, but always be mindful of which stage you are at in recovery. Otherwise, their issues can bring you to another downward spiral, one which we all try to avoid. Usually getting involved in what they're going through can help you forget your own issues. You don't have to come brazenly forward stating "I know what you're going through, I've been there." Well no, none of us know for certain what the other person is going through, only God knows. The simple act of a good morning smile, a warm hug, or just being a sounding board can make a world of difference in someone's life. It may even make a very positive impact on your own.

Speaking of helping others my friends, a very dear couple are involved in a program called "Reining Warriors." It is a nonprofit organization that assists Veterans and First Responders deal with witnessing the tragic events that oftentimes can lead to PTSD. My friend, a combat veteran, decided to give back and honor those friends he had lost to the illness. PTSD or Post Traumatic Stress Disorder is becoming an epidemic among American service men and women. I realize PTSD can also result from circumstances other than combat and is a growing concern with the general population as well. This organization, which my friends are passionate about, involve two things I hold very near and dear to my heart. Our veterans and God's amazing creation the horse. These folks have the innate ability to use equine therapy to reach an otherwise forgotten population in order to help them heal. According to some very frightening statistics twenty- two Veterans, five first responders, and one active duty service member take their lives daily in our country. The current systems we have in place are letting these remarkable human beings "slip through the cracks" so to speak, without the help they deserve. Their mission at the RW program is "To Heal with Horses." They provide hands on support for our servicemen, servicewomen, and first responders through a specific equine assisted program that provides training in equine care, management, groundwork, lessons, and horseback riding. Reining Warriors is about horses healing heroes. Horsemanship allows the participant to "drop their guard" and be open to learning about themselves as they learn from the horse. I love this program because they are so dedicated to give back and to help those who have served or are serving. A reverent act of service and recognition for those who have honored this great country.

If you happen not to be a "horse person," let me explain something. I know some of you are probably intimidated by the size of the animal, or perhaps you just don't see what we horse lovers see as an attraction. It's laughable how we can be so in love with a twelve-hundred-pound creature, kissing those soft muzzles, and then yelling at them to move out of the way when they block the stall at feeding time. It is truly a connection that must be so hard for those of you who weren't born with this innate desire to be around these remarkable creatures to even comprehend. For those of us who experience it for ourselves, it is very difficult to explain. It's a feeling of comfort to look deeply in those pools of liquid brown eyes. It calms the soul brushing away the dirt, the sweat and the tangles from their manes and tails. It's the art of moving those large creatures both from the ground and in the saddle, that gives you a sense of belonging. It's the ability of getting the horse to work in conjunction with yourself and your movements that makes you feel empowered and so free. Even mucking stalls, feeding hay, cleaning hooves, and all the other chores related to horsemanship can be therapy after a troubling day. The mind can somehow become immersed in this type of setting, forgetting all the circumstances surrounding the angst and anxiety in one's life. Of course, remaining vigilant due to the animal being five times your size will keep you on-your-toes and focused on the task at hand. All of this and more make the equine therapy programs an excellent alternative to the other means of treatment in the case of PTSD. Be mindful and support those type of programs and others if you can. Beyond a shadow of a doubt, you will see what kind of a difference you will make in the lives of those brave men and women.

I want to encourage each and every one of you to find your passion. Whether it's a previous activity you once loved, or something brand spanking new, don't be afraid to try it. You may be able to rekindle that fire that you once felt. It doesn't have to be sky diving or whitewater rafting. It can be as simple as knitting, or even teaching others how to. New passions can spring up even as one ages. Another friend of mine is a huge animal lover like me, and she ran our local Humane Society for many years. She was in her mid to late fifties before she found the benefits of equine therapy. She purchased and helped train her two young Morgan horses, and now at sixty-eight has become quite the accomplished horse woman. Find your passion and help others find theirs. You may just find out your passion or your therapy, is just plain helping. Jesus first, Yourself last, Others in between.

"And the Lord make you to increase and abound in love one toward another, and toward all men, even as we do toward you": (1 Thessalonians3:12)

CHAPTER 21

IN THE GARDEN

We have come to the final chapter in this short revelation, my testimony to an Almighty God, the Father of all creation. Given my Baptist background we never wrap up any event without giving what we call an invitation. In short, it is a means of welcoming those convicted by the Holy Spirit to the throne of God for reconciliation and then adoption so to speak. It can also be a time of re-dedication for those of us who have already been saved and perhaps maybe strayed from the path of God's will. The Bible gives us two options, to serve God or to serve ourselves. For those of you who think serving yourselves sounds like the better option, then be warned. Serving yourself really means you are serving the father of this world of sin, Satan. We all know the outcome for that choice and trust me we all want to avoid it at all cost. Knowing that, I want my readers to come to know the Lord as their personal Savior, to feel that close connection for themselves.

I began thinking what example from the Word of God could I use to tie into my theme: "trusting God in fearful and misleading times of anxiety and depression." I thought about titling this chapter as "The Cross," simply because that's how we come by salvation in the first place. Jesus, that precious perfect lamb of

God sacrificed himself there to cover our sin. It made perfect sense at first, but then I remembered something. Our Savior Jesus Christ in his human form experienced that fear, that anxiety, that painful expression of mind-altering darkness for himself. "What?" The Son of God, the mighty and powerful portion of the Trinity who can do all things? Ultimately, we're talking about a man who could heal lepers, cast out devils, and stop the raging seas, he felt anxiety? The answer is yes, our supreme example Jesus Christ. When, might you ask? Jesus the Son of God admittingly felt fear and trembling when he was in the garden, the garden of Gethsemane, only hours before the cross.

"Then cometh Jesus with them unto a place called Gethsemane, and saith unto the disciples, Sit ye here, while I go and pray yonder. And he took with him Peter and the two sons of Zebedee, and began to be sorrowful and very heavy. Then saith he unto them, My soul is exceeding sorrowful, even unto death: tarry ye here, and watch with me. And he went a little further, and fell on his face, and prayed, saying, O my Father, if it be possible, let this cup pass from me: nevertheless not as I will, but as thou wilt." (Matthew 26:36-39) "Sorrowful, heavy, exceeding sorrowful even unto death," all feelings that those of us experiencing this affliction can identify with. Of course, it's hard to make a true comparison because none of us are facing torture and certain death as Jesus was. The Bible goes on to say, Jesus felt the physical symptoms of anxiety and extreme stress as well. In the gospel of Luke chapter 22, verse 44; "And being in an agony he prayed more earnestly: and his sweat was as it were great drops of blood falling down to the ground." How many of us can claim ever being in such a state that we literally sweat drops of blood? That leads me to know our Savior, Jesus Christ, being the perfect Son of God, experienced an anxiety ridden, stress induced state that none of us can ever imagine. The Son who knew no sin, felt anxiety over the death that was coming. Proof positive that anxiety is not always sin, but a part of the humanistic side of our God made flesh. Jesus, as you know, overcame that anxiety and went willingly on to the cross as His Father God planned it. He conquered that fear. He then went on to conquer death, hell, and the grave when He arose again on that third day. Without this event none of us would have the hope of dwelling with Him in a place called Heaven. Fortunately, we will never know the type of fear or sorrow that Jesus did. Dying on the cross as both a guiltless human and God, Jesus felt the extreme agony and unending sorrow inflicted by the Romans. Knowing that He was dying, not because of his own sin, but because of ours, had to be the most devastating factor of it all.

The death of an innocent Jesus reminds me of another time in my life when God caused me to have a realization of this very thing. I was a young nurse, full of enthusiasm. I had begun working in the very department that I now manage, outpatient surgery. It had been a particularly stressful week that week. Not only were we busy at work, but there had been a death of a very close friend of the family. By the time Friday had rolled around, I was feeling very stressed, not to mention physically tired from all the activity. I can remember one of our patients, a familiar lady who visited us frequently and suffered from a debilitating illness, was under our care that day. The poor soul had been having an unusually painful bout of the affliction and needed treatment. She had what we call a porta Cath, or what we now know as a Power Port. A permanent indwelling device that is attached surgically to the large vena cava in the anterior chest wall. This device enables patients to obtain multiple treatments such as chemotherapy, over an extended time period. The purpose of this device is also saving these patients from multiple painful IV sticks each time they pay a visit. The porta Cath needles are very sharp, large bore, and somewhat short in length. They can range in sizes referred to as gauges, as well as shapes either straight or slightly bent. It takes skill to manage insertion in the exact area the needle must be placed under the skin. I was able to insert the catheter and give the correct dosage of the needed medication without error. The problem came however, while removing the access needle. As I held the device stable with my left hand, I gently grasped the hub of the needle and pulled it out. As I slowly removed the sharp, I wasn't paying close attention and grazed my left thumb. I quickly secured the patient's device, knowing full well that I had just stuck myself with a "dirty needle." A friend and fellow nurse witnessed the event and came to my aid. "Squeeze it," she said as we are taught to do as an attempt to remove the contamination. I did so, then quickly washed and disinfected the area. Fear immediately set in. As I stated before she was a familiar patient and one that I knew had once been addicted to drugs and alcohol. Given her history, I also knew that she was at high risk for having HIV or Hepatitis. If you are aware of bloodborne pathogens, you know these two dreaded diseases are acquired through tainted needles or simply being in contact with someone's blood or body fluid. I then followed protocol and went to the emergency room for testing, the patient herself was tested as well. Then it was a waiting game. Several days I was kept on "pins and needles" literally waiting for the results to become final. I prayed and pleaded for God to intervene. "Lord, why is it fair that I a non-drug user, should I have to suffer the consequences for someone who chose to make those mistakes in life?" The answer came resounding back to me, as plainly as I'm speaking now. "Roberta, isn't that what my Son did for you?" I immediately bowed my head. I had to admit that is exactly what Jesus did on that cross for me. I have sinned, I have made mistakes, but his death and resurrection had set me free. Who am I to judge this dear lady, who am I to say I shouldn't have to pay the penalty of her past failures, when I have so many myself? "God forgive me for my oversight," I prayed. "I will learn to trust you no matter the outcome."

As you may have already guessed the test results all came back negative, and I breathed a sigh of relief. God had gotten me out of yet another jam, and He has done so time and time again. I'm so very thankful, both for the protection, and for the lessons themselves. "Behold, happy is the man whom God correcteth: therefore despise not thou the chastening of the Almighty." (Job 5:17) Trials come no matter what, our job is to be ready to face them head on with God's help. For example, let's look at the sincere man of God, Job. If anyone had reason to suffer depression, it was he. Losing all ten children, his livestock, and his servants, he was left to sit in ashes and mourn. A once wealthy individual, you might say he lost everything thanks to Satan trying to prove a point. Satan accused God of building a protective hedge around Job, a dedicated servant. Satan challenged God, by saying" if I take away all he has he will surely turn against You." God allowed Satan to take all but Job's life itself. Job's wife even added insult to injury by telling her husband, "curse God and die!" Thankfully, Job did not listen to his wife, his friends, or the evil Satan, he remained steady in his faith even through all that grief. He claimed in Job 1:21; "Naked came I out of my mother's womb, and naked shall I return thither: the Lord gave, and the Lord hath taken away; blessed be the name of the Lord." How many of us would make that proclamation after such a tragic loss? I shudder to think what my reaction would be. I would hope that through all my hardships, I would have learned to accept, let go, and let God. That should be the hope for all of us as Christians. Even those of us who experience the affliction of anxiety and depression should hold that knowledge near and dear to our hearts. Let God have the control, focus on Him, and He will give you the comfort you need.

If you are currently struggling with a mental health crisis, I encourage you to please seek help. It doesn't matter what your peers say, your fellow church members, your family, especially if they are using negative reinforcement. "Don't go see that doctor, you can get through this, God will help," "You don't need that medicine, all you need is the Lord." Truth is you do need God, but as I've explained, God needs you to understand He works in a variety of ways. His ways are higher than our ways, remember that. Salvation comes to those who depend upon the Lord. I plead with you to be your own mental health advocate, acquire counseling, accept therapy, in order to obtain peace of mind. These are the small simple rantings of an old country girl hoping to reach fellow believers whether you are a Baptist or not. Acknowledging that the pain of anxiety and depression is real and that no matter what anyone says we have a loving God who can heal through the works of others. Keep in mind He is a God who does not condemn those of us who suffer from this mental illness and deep despondency. As Christians we know there is comfort in God's word, the Holy Bible. Prayer, along with the action of serving others can go along way during those dark times in the life of a Christian.

If you are an unbeliever, I want to offer you the benefit of serving a mighty Savior. I myself cannot save you. I can only hope I've helped you see your need for a loving God. One last take away from a long time Sunday school attendee; A=Admit that you are a sinner; B=Believe Jesus Christ the only Son of God died on the cross for your sin; C=Confess your sins are forgiven and Commit to God.

Romans Road:

"For all have sinned, and come short of the glory of God." (Romans 3:23)

"For the wages of sin is death; but the gift of God is eternal life through Jesus Christ our Lord." (Romans 6:23)

"But God demonstrates His own love toward us, in that while we were still sinners, Christ died for us." (Romans 5:8)

"That if you confess with your mouth Jesus as Lord, and believe in your heart that God raised Him from the dead, you will be saved." (Romans 10:9)

"For Everyone who calls on the name of the Lord will be saved." (Romans 10:13)

"Therefore, since we have been justified through faith, we have peace with God through our Lord Jesus Christ." (Romans 5:1)

God has chosen each of us for His specific purpose in this life. Overcoming the anxiety and depression the stress of this world can cause is difficult, but not impossible. Luke 18:27 tells us "The things which are impossible with men are possible with God." Please keep trying, keep going and do not give up under any circumstances. With certainty God is always with us. I will be praying for all of you and you please pray for me. In the words of my dear great-grandmother, "God be with you till we meet again."

(Psalms 30:5) "For his anger endureth but a moment; in his favour is life: weeping may endure for a night, but joy cometh in the morning."

CPSIA information can be obtained
at www.ICGtesting.com
Printed in the USA
BVHW082046050820
585578BV00003B/230